Donna Myer

Answers to your Mushroom Questions plus Recipes

Answers to your Mushroom Questions plus Recipes
by Donna Myer

Copyright © Donna Myer 1977
All rights reserved.
Inquiries should be addressed to Donna Myer,
Box 894, Battle Creek, Michigan, 49016.

Printed in the United States of America
by E.P.I. Printers

Library of Congress Catalog Card Number: 77-087780
International Standard Book Number: 0-9601516-1-3
First Edition

Photocover by L. West

Illustrations by Gail Guth

Acknowledgments

The author is grateful for permission to reprint extracts from the following books, articles and speeches:

ALL COLOR BOOK OF MUSHROOMS AND FUNGI by Moira Savonius, Crescent Books

AMANA® RADARANGE ® MICROWAVE OVEN COOK BOOK, 1975, Amana Refrigeration, Inc.

Assorted Readings from PROCEEDINGS OF SEMINAR ON MUSHROOM RESEARCH AND PRODUCTION, Pakistan Press

BEYOND PYRAMID POWER by Pat Flanagan, DeVorss & Co.

DON'T PICK POISON by Ingrid Bartelli, Cooperative Extension Service, Michigan State University

MAY IS MOREL MONTH IN MICHIGAN by Ingrid Bartelli, Cooperative Extension Service, Michigan State University

MUSHROOM COOKERY by Rosetta Reitz, Gramercy Publishing Co., Walker and Company, New York, 1945

MUSHROOM GROWING AND THE MUSROOM INDUSTRY by Aron Kinrus, American Mushroom Institute

MUSHROOM GROWING TO-DAY by R. C. Atkins, Faber and Faber

THE MUSHROOM HUNTER'S FIELD GUIDE by Alexander H. Smith, University of Michigan Press, 1963, The University of Michigan

MUSHROOMS AND PENN STATE, PAST, PRESENT, FUTURE by Robert Snetsinger, Penn State University

"Mushrooms as a Source of Food Protein" by Ralph H. Kurtzman from PROTEIN NUTRITIONAL QUALITY OF FOODS AND FEEDS

MUSHROOMS GROW ON STUMPS by Ingrid Bartelli, Cooperative Extensive Service, Michigan State University

MUSHROOMS MOULDS AND MIRACLES by Lucy Kavaler, Geo. G. Harrap and Company

1001 QUESTIONS ANSWERED ABOUT TREES by Rutherford Platt, Dodd, Mead and Company

RICHARD DEACON MICROWAVE COOKBOOK by Richard Deacon, Thermador/Waste King

THE SACRED MUSHROOM AND THE CROSS by John Allegro, Hodder and Stroughton, Ltd.

WILD MUSHROOM COOKERY, The Oregon Mycological Society, Inc.

WILD MUSHROOM RECIPES by Members of Puget Sound Mycological Society, Pacific Search

A special thanks to James P. San Antonio and Ralph H. Kurzman of the United States Department of Agriculture, for their invaluable assistance in locating the unlocatable.

Illustration from
"Our Edible Toadstools and Mushrooms"

Contents

Mushroom	Page
1 Description	15
2 Preparation	23
3 Growing	29
4 Consumption	36
5 Wild	39
6 Poisonous	48
7 Miscellaneous	52
8 Loose Ends	56
9 Recipes	58
Bibliography	73
Index	75

x

Foreword

People in Battle Creek refer to me as The Mushroom Lady because for five years I have rushed fresh mushrooms from the mushroom farm to their door. This book is an answer to their many questions plus some of my own.

As I searched for answers through the years, it became apparent that most books available at book stores and libraries were aimed at the identification of wild mushrooms and a few at how to grow commercial mushrooms. Thus, I decided to collect questions and answers to cover the general subjects for all mushroom lovers and students.

The information printed here, for your enjoyment and enlightenment, has been collected from books, trade magazines, pamphlets, government bulletins and reports, conversations with experts, letters, and personal experiences. If this booklet doesn't answer all your questions, perhaps it can guide you to literature or people who can.

I would appreciate any additional mushroom information which you would care to share with me. If you want an answer please enclose a self-addressed, stamped envelope.

        Donna Myer
        Post Office Box 894
        Battle Creek, Michigan 49016

Answers to your Mushroom Questions plus Recipes

DESCRIPTION

1. **What are mushrooms?** The dictionary says a mushroom is "Any of the various rapid-growing fleshy fungi having a stalk with an umbrella-like top. That 'umbrella' shape can vary from cone, trumpet or button; its texture can be smooth, spongy or warted."

Fungi have no green coloring (chlorophyll), thus they cannot take carbon dioxide from the air to manufacture carbohydrates. They breathe by taking in oxygen and exhaling carbon dioxide, the opposite process from ordinary plant life. They also give off the metabolic gases of ethylene, acetaldehyde, acetone, ethyl alcohol, and ethyl acetate. (31) Mushrooms are the most advanced form of fungi.

Fungi have three types of relationships with their environment.
  1. Parasitic—live directly on living organisms without benefiting their host.
  2. Saprophytic—live on dead material such as compost.
  3. Mycorrihizal—Symbiotic—growing on the roots of a green plant, but not destroying it. They each supply certain chemicals or nutrients to the other.

The mushrooms are the fruit of the plant which is under cover in the soil, stumps, piles of straw or leaf mold. That is why mushrooms seem to appear from nowhere. Their bodies die and decay soon after releasing their spores (seeds), but the vegetative mycelia which produced them generally live on to produce successive crops of fruiting bodies and are potentially immortal.

2. **What are the parts of a mushroom?** Cap (pileus); gills (lamelai) under cap, spores are released from this area; veil (allulus) stretches across the bottom of the cap area—forms the collar; stem (stipe); cup (volva) holds mushroom; roots (mycelium). Your mushroom identification book will describe/illustrate these parts for the various species. Not all are present in each mushroom.

3. **What are the stages in the development of the cultivated mushroom?** Pinhead, closed, open, flat.

4. **How does a mushroom grow?** The life cycle of a mushroom has three stages: 1. the spores or seeds, 2. the mycelium or spawn growth (like cob webs) and 3. the fruit (mushrooms). Wild mushrooms have the ability to skip the fruiting stage of their life cycle. If growing conditions are not favorable for a year or more they can still survive.

5. **Are mushrooms a vegetable?** People think of them as a vegetable but they are a fungus. Vegetables are plants. Plants manufacture their own food; mushrooms, being a fungus, cannot. They must depend upon organic matter for nutrition.

6. **How do mushrooms reproduce?** When a mushroom matures it releases millions of spores (seeds). A single spore is so tiny you need a pile of them to tell what color they are. You check their color by taking a spore print. (See Q90.)

If temperature, moisture and soil are just right the spores produce a threadlike mass called mycelium, which in turn, if conditions are right, will develop mushrooms.

Animals enjoy eating mushrooms, and the spores pass through them unharmed. The animal dung provides an excellent place for them to germinate. Insects, flys and slugs also provide transportation for the spores.[4]

Commercial mushroom farms purchase or grow their own mycelium in laboratories which grow pure cultures on special media. In practice today milo or grain sorgum, millet, or rye are generally used as the grain. Chalk or ground limestone is added at about two percent of the dry weight of the grain, and it is cooked in water much as one cooks rice. The cooked grain is then put in bottles, the bottles covered with cotton or some other material through which air can easily pass, and then they are autoclaved (sterilized in a commercial pressure cooker at 15 psi) for several hours, depending on the size of the bottle. After the bottles have cooled they are inoculated with mushroom mycelium. After the spawn is fully grown (requires from two to four weeks to grow) it may be put in paper bags to make it easier to ship.[13]

At the farm the spawn is mixed throughout the compost as evenly as possible at a rate of one to two ounces per square foot.[13]

7. **What is the mushroom's place in nature's plan?** The purpose of fungi is to bring about the decay of dead plants and animals and their waste products. (11) The mycelium (threads) do the actual work of eating, that is breaking down, all the organic debris. "The threads exude the enzymes which digest food material outside the body of the thread. When the digested material is in solution it is absorbed by the threads and used in the life processes of the fungus, some of it eventually being used to produce mushrooms."[30] We owe them a debt of gratitude for providing us with an orderly place to live.

What we call the mushroom is really the fruit (carpophore or sporophore) of a fungus. The fungus itself, the mycelium, is buried underground, in bark, manure or other organic matter.

The mushroom's function is to produce the spores.

8. **What is the difference between mushrooms and toadstools?** People generally refer to edible species as mushrooms and poisonous ones as toadstools. There is no scientific distinction between the two.

The word toadstool is used in informal conversation. The fact that toads are attracted to mushrooms by the many insects gathered there probably has contributed to the name.

9. **How did the mushroom get its name?** Middle English for "mushroom" was "muscheron"; Old French was "moucheron" or "mouseron," [32] meaning softness, sponginess of texture; [21] apparently derived from "mousse," the word for moss, of Teutonic origin. Latin for moss was "muscus" and Old Slav was "muchu."[27]

10. **How do scientists classify mushrooms into groups?** They are classified according to the way the spores are produced. Morel spores are produced in a pod-like structure called an ascus so they are called ASCOMYCETES. Other mushrooms produce spores on a club-shaped structure known as a basidium. This large group of mushrooms is called BASIDIOMYCETES.[6] They include the commercial *Agaricus bisporus.*

In mushroom descriptions you will see several botanical (Latin) names. The first is the name of the group (genus) to which the mushroom belongs (Capitalized). The second part of the name is called the species epithet (not capitalized).

Collectors should learn the Latin names which have specific meaning rather than the common nicknames. The Latin names are known worldwide, although sometimes the same species is classified by one author under one genus and under another by a different author.

11. **How many different kinds of mushrooms are there in the U. S. and Canada?** Depending upon which expert you quote, somewhere between 2,000 and 3,000. These include agarics (gill fungi), boletes (tube fungi), clavarias (coral fungi), earth stars, hydnums (teeth fungi), polypores (pore, or bracket fungi), puffballs, stinkhorn and bird's nest fungi, morels, and cup fungi.

12. **What is the U. S. commercial mushroom's botanical name?** The *Agaricus bisporus,* the only commercially grown mushroom in the United States, is also grown throughout the world. They are specifically distinct from the field mushroom, *Agaricus* (or *Psalliota*) *campestris,* and the horse mushroom, *Agaricus* or *Psalliota avbensis* because the wild bear their spores in groups of four, the cultivated usually in two's.[4]

The position of the cultivated mushroom in the classification of plants is as follows:

Kingdom: Third
Division: Thallophyta
Subdivision: Fungi
Class: Eumycetes
Order: Basidiomycetes
Family: Agaricaceae
Species: Agaricus bisporus

13. **What is our commercial mushroom's common name?** "The economic importance of this species has been so great relative to other mushrooms, that it has never been given a really usable common name. Some of those used are the mushroom, our mushroom, champignon, button mushroom, white mushroom, and champignon de Paris. For lack of a better name, we prefer to call it the common commercial mushroom of the West."[13]

14. **Where can I find mushrooms growing?** Anywhere, when the weather conditions are right. Some type of mushroom grows in all types of land: deserts, forests, fields, or tundra.

15. **Which mushrooms are the most popular for eating?** Most American mushroom lovers are familiar only with the commercial mushroom *Agaricus bisporus*. The next most familiar probably is the wild morel (sponge), followed by puffballs and shaggymanes. Many people gather the wild *Agaricus campestris* but since the deadly Amantis is so easy to confuse with it even experts make mistakes.

16. **What are the other mushrooms grown commercially in other countries?**
    Flammulina velutipes—Winter Mushroom, Enotake
       Japanese—grown in bottles on sawdust and rice bran, fruits from 32° to 60° F. (It is second to Shiitake in production in Japan.)
    Pleurotus ostreatus and *P. sapidus*—Oyster mushrooms
       Is sold in Europe for twice the price of *Agaricus*, but the market is apparently not strong. Keeps well with refrigeration, can be canned and dries well. Grows on straw, paper, sawdust and logs. 50° to 70° F., humidity 85%, needs light
    Pleurotus cornucopiae—Tamogitake
       Japanese
    Pholiota nameko—Nameko
       Japanese—grows on blocks of wood, out-of-doors in late autumn
    Lentinus edodes—Shiitake
       Japan—second most important mushroom in world commerce—normally preserved by drying, often referred to as "The Chinese mushroom." When the sun is used for drying, vitamin D is produced. It is grown on logs, particularly Quercus, Pasania, Fagus, and other Fagales. 60° to 75° F. Until recently it was always grown out-of-doors. Light is required, so if Shiitake is grown in buildings, either windows or artificial light must be provided. The advantage of buildings in regulating conditions has been of great value. (Now being grown in California.)

Auricularia auricula—Judea, Judas Ear, Senji, Cloud's Ear
Japan—Taiwan—favored for its crisp texture generally sold dried—grown on sawdust and rice bran or mango logs. 75° to 79° F.

Tremella fuciformis—White Jelly, Snow Fungus
Taiwan and Japan—The Chinese make a sweet soup or a hot punch with it and pineapple or other fruit juice.

Pleurotus cystidiosus—Tropical Oyster Mushroom
Taiwan—sawdust and rice bran—75° to 79° F.

Agaricus bitorquis
This mushroom is apparently much like *Agaricus bisporus* except that it is larger, better keeping, and grows at a higher temperature—73° to 79° F.

Volvariella volvacae—Padi Straw Mushroom, Chinese Mushroom
It is cultivated from Thailand to the Philippines. It does not keep well fresh but cans well. Grows on rice straw with supplements or on cotton wastes. 77° to 90° F.—humidity must be maintained at over 85% —light required.[13]

17. **How are commercial mushrooms graded?** The U. S. Department of Agriculture (USDA) has a classification system that embraces three grades: No. 1 grade has the best appearance, the mildest flavor, and the highest price; No.2 grade is intermediate; No. 3 grade, the most mature of the three, is lowest in price, the least attractive in appearance, and, in the opinion of many persons, the best in taste.

In the U. S. the majority of the growers' output of the No. 1 grade goes to the fresh market.

18. **What is the season for mushrooms?** The mushroom crop depends mainly upon the weather, temperature in particular. The best commercial mushroom temperatures range between 50° and 60° F. Wild mushrooms, of course, are forced to develop a greater tolerance for both high and low temperatures. To much or too little water prevents or slows mushroom growth. Most wild mushrooms appear in the coolness of early spring and in late summer and autumn. Commercial mushrooms grow year around, but also are at their best during cool weather.

19. **Are there different colored commercially grown mushrooms?** Yes, spawn laboratories offer white, off-white, cream and brown spawn (all are *Agaricus bisporus)* to the United States mushroom growers.

20. **What are the nutritional values of mushrooms?** Views ex-

pressed about the nutritional value of mushrooms have ranged from calling them "vegetable beefsteak," which they are not, to saying they have virtually no food value and are good only for flavoring, which also is not true.[27]

Different mushroom species vary in their composition and nutritive value.[13]

According to the USDA Handbook #8, December, 1963, the cultivated mushroom has the following composition per 100 grams (3.5 ounces) edible portion, uncooked:

Water	90.4%	Sodium	15 mg.
Calories	28	Potassium	414 mg.
Protein	2.7 grams	Vitamin A	trace
Fat	.3 g.	Thiamine	0.10 mg.
Total Carbohydrate	4.4 g.	Riboflavin	0.46 mg.
Ash	.9 g.	Niacin	4.2 mg.
Calcium	6 milligrams	Ascorbic acid	3 mg.
Phosphorus	116 mg.	Magnesium	13 mg.
Iron	.8 mg.		

Additional trace minerals are given in Albritton's Standard Values in Nutrition and Metabolism as follows: Trace mineral content, per 100 grams edible portion of uncooked mushrooms:

Chlorine	21 mg.	Sulfur	34 mg.
Copper	1.79 mg.	Zinc	0.28 mg.
Manganese	0.08 mg.		

Mushrooms are an excellent source of folic acid, the blood-building vitamin which counteracts pernicious anemia. They also contain trypsin which is an ensyme valuable as an aid to digestion and are a diuretic which makes the body pass off more water.

Working with mushrooms, Japanese investigators have isolated "eritadenine," a chemical, which lowers cholesterol in blood.[17]

Fresh mushrooms, on the basis of their known nutrient content, deserve a respected place in the well-balanced diet for their positive contribution of nutrients over and above their value for adding flavor and zest to other foods.

"When mushrooms (cultivated) were fed as the sole source of protein to white rats, they survived and grew, although not to the same extent as did rats which were fed casein or soybean meal. From the results of the animal feeding experiments it was concluded that all of the essential amino acids are present in mushrooms but in lower concentrations than are found in casein. Chemical analyses showed that about 63% of the total nitrogen of mushrooms is in the form of protein."[9]

21. **What are the different kinds of edible mushrooms on the market?** Only one mushroom, *Agaricus bisporus,* has been de-

veloped as a cultivated mushroom in the U. S. The white varieties which are found in groceries today are all descendants of a clump of white ones a Pennsylvania farmer found in his bed of cream *A. bisporus* back in 1926.[11] The other colored ones are mainly used for canning.

Many kinds of European and Oriental mushrooms are available at speciality or foreign grocery stores, either in cans or dried. Three outstanding European mushrooms are the Morel, Cepes and the Chanterelle. The mushroom that is dried in Europe is generally the *Boletus edulis* (Cepes). The Morel also grows wild in the U. S. It has a short season and is expensive to buy (See Q102). Morels have cone-shaped caps which look like sponges and range in color from tan to dark brown. Cepes are large, strongly-flavored mushrooms ranging in color from yellow to reddish-brown. They come in cans or dried. Chanterelles are cup-shaped with frilly edges and shallow gills of a pale or dark yellow color. Oriental mushrooms are Mutsutake, a fragrant Japanese mushroom available in the U. S. dried or canned, and Shiitake, a Japanese "tree mushroom" available in the U. S. dried and occasionally fresh (California grown).

22. **What are the different ways you can purchase mushrooms?** Fresh at the market or dried mushrooms which come into this country hermetically packed in boxes or bags. Most dried mushrooms are reprocessed in food factories or used in hotels and large restaurants or in mix packages. Frozen mushrooms are available at frozen food departments, mainly mixed in with other vegetables. Canned mushrooms are available as caps, slices, chopped or whole, with or without butter, pickled, and coarsely cut pieces of stems and caps.

23. **What about imported canned mushrooms?** Most of the imported canned mushrooms are of the same species as those grown in the U. S. and are comparable in flavor and appearance to them. Virtually all of the imports from Taiwan, South Korea, and France and most of the imports from Japan are of this species. A small portion of them, however, consist of either cultivated or wild species not grown commercially in the U. S. and are different from the domestic cultivated mushroom in flavor and appearance. The most important of these is the Shiitake mushroom from Japan, which is used principally in oriental cuisine.[19] Frequently, because of tradition, fancy packaging, and reputed quality, mushrooms imported from France have a prestige value over the domestic product. They are sold principally to restaurants and gourmet food stores, where consumers are willing to pay a higher price for them.[19] The ones most frequently found in specialty or large department stores are the Cep *(Boletus edulis)* and the Chanterelle *(Cantharellus cibarius)*. They will generally be labeled

with their country of origin and Latin name. Generally a can will have a picture label of its contents.

24. **What is the foreign translation for cep** *(Boletus edulis)*?
    cepe—France
    steinpilz—Germany
    steinpilz—Switzerland
    herrenpilz—Austria
    porcino—Italy
    baroviki—Poland
    belya-grib—Russia
    stensopp—Denmark [24]

25. **What is the foreign translation for chanterelle**
    Chanterelle—France
    Chanterelle—Switzerland
    Girolle—France
    pfefferling—Germany
    vanlig kantarell—Sweden [24]

PREPARATION

26. **How long do mushrooms keep after they are picked?** This depends upon the temperature, the humidity and the physical treatment they receive. If they are handled gently, stored where it is 35° to 40° F., and not allowed to sweat (they do this in a closed plastic bag or with a change in temperature), Commercial mushrooms may keep as long as two weeks. If care is not taken with them they can spoil in one day, especially in hot weather. The low temperature increases their life by lowering the respiration rate. Wild mushrooms should be cooked or processed the same day as they are picked.

27. **How do you store mushrooms?** Refrigerate them immediately since they are highly perishable once they are picked. Place in a shallow pan or tray, cover with moistened paper toweling (not dripping wet) and store so air will circulate around them. The middle rack in your refrigerator is better than the top or bottom one. Do not try to store them in an airtight plastic container; condensation will ruin them.

28. **Which size mushroom is the best?** The commercial mushroom is picked at different stages and can have a cap as small as ¾ of an inch or as wide as 4 inches. Button, as the small ones are called, have closed caps (the gills do not show on the bottoms of the caps). Their stems are short. Mature mushrooms have caps which have opened so you can see the gills exposed. The older they are the darker brown the gills. The texture of the two is a little different but the flavor is the same. Since size really makes no difference, how you want to use them would determine the size you need. WILD: The unripe or medium ripe are the best. They generally are not as insect-infested as the more mature specimens. Mushrooms, like other fruit, continue to mature even after they are picked.

29. **What is the preferred store packaging?** Mushrooms displayed on grocers' shelves loose and uncovered in large boxes or baskets suffer from much handling. Most chain stores prefer prepackaged mushrooms. Mushrooms packed in small boxes at the Mushroom Farm are tightly packed without being forced, to prevent abrasion bruises, and covered with a gas-permeable film so mushrooms can breath.[27]

30. **Why do mushrooms in the store look so bad most of the time?** Most groceries do not keep them in a cool enough display case. Remember they keep best at around 32°. Much experimentation has been done to try to extend the shelf life of mushrooms. One thing that has proven to be of great value is vacuum cooling immediately when they are picked.

31. **Why do mushrooms cost so much?** Mushrooms are a perishable crop which requires a lot of hand labor and expensive, closely regulated temperatures. The mushroom grower's profit depends upon the success of the crop. Because production yields are highly variable it is difficult for a grower to estimate his cost. Prices differ from one locality to another and from one season to another. Fortunately canning industries have served as a stabilizing force on the price.[12] As a rule price does not have anything to do with the quality of the mushroom. Evaporation is a costly problem to both wholesalers and grocers. Mushrooms are around 90% water and considerable evaporation occurs during transportation and in the display cases. Each pound of water evaporated equals one pound of mushrooms not sold. The high price of fuel affects the mushroom price since such large quantities of it are needed to air-condition the growing sheds and transportation trucks. Mushrooms need large quantities of water, also an expensive item.

In large cities produce dealers sell mushrooms on consignment, setting the wholesale price by supply and demand and collecting a 10% commission on sales. Large city newspapers generally print the daily wholesale price of fresh mushrooms.[16]

As prices rise on other vegetables mushroom prices become competitive for the shoppers' fresh vegetable allowance. This encourages shoppers to use mushrooms as a complete dish rather than just a seasoning.

Consider the fact that mushrooms sold for $1.50 a pound in 1892.[31]

32. **How do you clean mushrooms?** COMMERCIAL: Do not peel mushrooms. Much of their flavor and nutritional value is in the skin. Commercial mushrooms are not generally very dirty so a damp cloth or paper towel or soft brush will wipe them clean. Wipe gently because they bruise very easily. If it is necessary to wash mushrooms, hold them in your hand, cap up, or put them in a container with holes in the bottom and run cold tap water over them, then wipe dry immediately. Never soak mushrooms because they absorb the water, then suddenly release it along with much of the mushroom flavor when they are cooked. Only wash mushrooms when you are ready to use them. WILD: As soon as you get home complete the cleaning of the mushrooms. Often the first thing people do is to put them into water. THIS IS A MISTAKE. Clean as for the commercial ones, cut them lengthwise from base to cap. Now you can see if anything is hiding inside. Fresh mushrooms should be rinsed, very quickly, only a few minutes before starting your meal, then dried immediately. Peel off the cap only if it is tough or very sticky and discard stems, which are usually tough.

33. **What is the best way to slice mushrooms?** Slice mushrooms

with the knife blade parallel to the stem and running through it. In this way you get larger slices and can get them as thin as wafers. Slicing them across renders the stems almost unusable. (15)

34. **How do you cook mushrooms?** COMMERCIAL: Mushrooms can be eaten raw (not recommended by food inspectors), sauted, broiled, boiled, baked, steamed or pickled. They are used in sauces, gravies, stuffings, stews, omelets, soups, salads, hamburgers, meatloaf and pizzas. WILD: Always prepare or process mushrooms immediately. Wild mushrooms vary in flavor and texture. The delicate-flavored ones are overpowered by garlic or strong-flavored spices. The firm or tougher mushrooms, such as the *Polyporus sulphureus*, require long and slow cooking.

The excellent paperback cookbook, *Wild Mushroom Recipes,* by the Puget Sound Mycological Society, published by Pacific Search, 715 Harrison Street, Seattle, Washington, 98109 ($6.95 + 75¢ postage and handling), covers the cooking of all types of wild mushrooms.

Many recipes call for sauted mushrooms. This removes the excess liquid so the completed dish is not watery or discolored.

35. **Why do cookbooks say not to soak mushrooms in water?** Mushrooms absorb water very quickly, then when heated, rapidly release it along with the mushrooms' flavor.

36. **Does it matter what kind of pan I use to cook mushrooms?** Cook mushrooms in a stainless steel or enamelware pan; aluminum sometimes causes discoloration of mushrooms.[24]

37. **What are the best mushroom seasonings?** Butter, olive oil, salt, pepper, ginger, nutmeg, lemon juice, paprika, shallots, chives, parsley, tarragon, marjoram, oregano and rosemary.

38. **How many calories are there in mushrooms?** From 66 to 90 per pound.

39. **How can I get a bargain on mushrooms?** If you live near mushroom farms find out if you can purchase directly from them. Some sell firsts (closed, #1), others only seconds (opens, flats, #2). Learn how to preserve mushrooms so that none go to waste when you have more than you can use or see them on special sales.

Cool nights and warm days in the spring raise the temperature in mushroom buildings. This temperature rise brings on more mushrooms and puts an excess on the market. Since they are so perishable prices sometimes drop.

You can become a wild mushroom collector and charge off to entertainment any expense you have.

40. **If a recipe calles for a certain measurement of canned mushrooms can you substitute fresh or dried ones?** Yes, substitute as follows:

   15 ozs. fresh mushrooms ....3 ozs. dried mushrooms
   1 pound fresh mushrooms ....1 eight ounce can
   ½ pound fresh mushrooms ....1 four ounce can
   20 to 24 fresh medium caps ....1 eight ounce can
   1 quart fresh mushrooms.......................1 eight ounce can

41. **Why do mushrooms shrink so much while cooking?** They release as much as 40% of their weight in liquid while they cook. They are nearly 90% water.

42. **Should stems be discarded?** Commercial: No. If you are using caps only in a recipe, save the stems. Slice or mince them and use for flavoring in soups, sauces, hamburgers, gravies or vegetables. They are handy to have waiting in the freezer. Wild: Yes, generally they are tough.

43. **Why do mushrooms turn dark color?** Mushroom tissue turns black due to the action of the oxydizing enzyme, polyphenol oxidase. Bruising or exposure to room temperature accelerates darkness; refrigeration slows the process.[27] Slightly discolored mushrooms are perfectly acceptable for cooking. As discoloration continues flavor and moisture will be lost but as long as the cap remains firm they are edible.

44. **How do you know when a mushroom is spoiled?** You can tell by looking at it. A good mushroom has a firm cap. When it is spoiled it looks slimy and watery throughout. Wild ones are soft and probably infested with insects.

45. **Does it hurt you to eat raw mushrooms?** Many people eat raw commercially grown mushrooms although official health food inspectors do not recommend eating them without cooking. Some wild mushrooms are actually poisonous when eaten raw. Check your identification book; know exactly what you are eating. Remember: Wild mushrooms generally have insect eggs in them which rapidly hatch into grubs.

46. **How do you freeze mushrooms?** When mushrooms are frozen raw they retain their full flavor for only about a month. They will keep much longer if blanched by steaming or boiling, or by being sauted before freezing.[12] The easiest way is: clean mushrooms, add ½ tsp. salt to 1 quart rapidly boiling water, add mushrooms (preferably sliced), boil 3 minutes, rinse mushrooms with cold water, drain thoroughly. Seal in an air tight container or bag.

Frozen mushrooms release lots of black liquid during thawing. They are fine for stews, sauces and soups where extra liquid isn't noticed. For use in other recipes thaw mushrooms and pat them dry.

You might consider putting the blanched mushrooms into your blender. Pour the sauce into muffin tins or ice cube trays, freeze and then bag. This is a good way to use stems. Since frozen mushrooms are inclined to be rubbery this is a way to use them for flavoring without noticing the texture. It is also a way to fool "fussy" eaters.

Commercial freezing is done by the instant quick freeze process using liquid nitrogen.

47. **How do you can mushrooms?** Cover mushrooms with cold water, let stand 10 minutes, drain, wash again. Heat mushrooms, but do not boil, for 15 minutes in just enough water to prevent sticking. Pack hot into hot jars, leaving 1" head space. Add ½ tsp. salt and ⅛ tsp. ascorbic acid to each pint. Add boiling water if needed to cover up to 1" headspace. Tighten lids, process pint or half pint jars at 10 pounds for 30 minutes. Do not use quarts. Do not water bath. Wild: Same as above. Be sure to trim stems, and cut away discolored parts.

48. **How are mushrooms canned in the factory?** Each day fresh-picked mushrooms are rushed from farm to cannery. When their temperatures are equalized they start on their way through the cannery. Trimmers remove the roots and separate the cap from the stem. Water carries the caps to tanks where they are washed and graded by size. They are blanched by either hot water or steam to shrink them (as much as 40% by weight). After a final inspection they travel to weighing stations where cans are filled and weighed and a salt or salt/acid brine is added. Next they are pressure-cooked, then travel to the shipping room, to the wholesaler, to the grocery and finally to your shelf.[12] In 1975/76, 83% of the U. S. produced mushrooms packed in brine consisted of stems and pieces, 8% sliced and 9% whole or buttons.[20]

49. **How do you dry mushrooms?** Do not wash mushrooms. Dirt washes out when you wash the dried mushrooms before cooking. Clean and scrape debris and dirt from the cap and stems. Slice ¼ inch thick.

   1.   String and hang in a light, airy room (or in the sun and breeze) or

   2.   Lay in single layers on papers and turn daily until they are thoroughly dry or

   3.   Dry on hardware cloth over a heat register or

   4.   Use a food dryer. When thoroughly dry, place in airtight containers sprinkled with black peppercorns or hang in paper bags in a warm, dry place such as near a furnace. Do not attempt to dry mushrooms in the oven. Mushrooms tend to cook and become tough.

When ready to use for cooking, wash in cold water, changing water 3-4 times. Let soak in cold water for 30 minutes or hot water for 15 minutes. Drain and use as fresh.[35]

Try drying mushrooms in a pyramid. Ask your bookstore or library for books which explain this process. *Beyond Pyramid Power,* G. Pat Flanagan, Devorss and Co., goes beyond the others in discussing "Experimentation has shown that there is a Critical Energy Ratio, or CER between the pyramid and the item to be treated. This ratio is based on the volume of the pyramid and the volume of the item to be treated. A pyramid of certain dimension only has a certain capacity. When the capacity of the pyramid is exceeded, the experiment is doomed to failure. The volume of the item to be treated MUST NOT EXCEED 5% OF THE VOLUME OF THE PYRAMID."[10] Pyramid energy slows or stops the growth of microorganisms which are responsible for spoilage.

50. **What is the source of dried mushroom powder?** Imports mostly, because their prices are lower than U. S. prices. Mainly U. S. mushrooms are dried in a vacuum, while frozen, by a firm in Pennsylvania and one in New York State.

During the market year 1975/76 we imported from various countries: Japan, 521,000 lbs.; Republic of China, 113,000 lbs.; Chile, 448,000 lbs.; France, 1,000 lbs.; West Germany, 22,000 lbs.; all others, 53,000 lbs. (Source: compiled from official statistics of the U. S. Dept. of Commerce) Note: 1 pound of dried mushrooms is equivalent to 10 pounds of fresh mushrooms.[20]

51. **How can you make mushroom powder?** Once the mushrooms are dried, they can be rubbed through a sieve or ground in an electric blender to make mushroom powder. Put powder in jars with airtight lids, and store in a cool dry place. Mushroom powder makes excellent flavoring for sauces, stews, soups, etc.

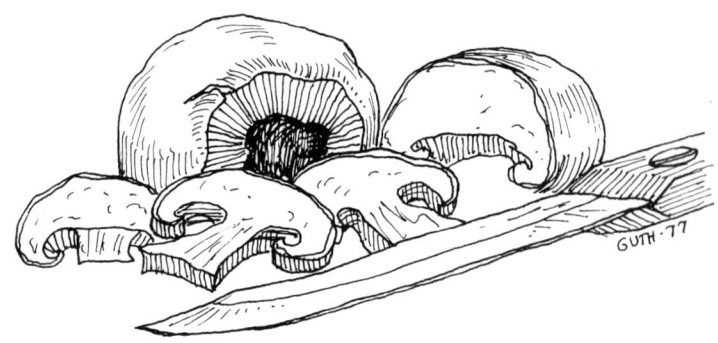

GROWING

52. What is the history of commercially grown mushrooms? Some unknown French person found a way of treating horse manure and planting wild mushroom spawn in it during the end of the seventeenth century. In 1707 a French publication described the growing procedure and around 1800 the French started growing mushrooms underground.

English growers specialized in supplying wild "brick spawn" to the rest of the world. Unfortunately, wild spawn was full of insects, mold, etc. To solve this problem the French, in 1894, succeeded in producing uncontaminated spawn from mushroom spores in a laboratory. In 1905 a man in the U. S. found a way to make pure spawn from mushroom tissue, using horse manure for its food supply. This new knowledge opened the way to select and guarantee a particular strain and the mushroom business began to develop into the highly scientific industry we know today.[4] But still there were problems associated with the use of manure for spawn. In 1932 Pennsylvania State University patented the use of grain to feed the spawn, resulting from research by their professor, Dr. Siden. This development eliminated growing problems and today's spawn is still grown in this manner.[3]

The first U. S. mushroom growers were around New York City where mushrooms were grown in cellars, caves, cisterns, and under greenhouse benches in the late 1800's. The greenhouse men around Phildelphia became so successful at growing mushrooms in their greenhouses they designed special buildings just for the mushrooms.[27]

Increased demand and market for mushrooms due to the growth of the canning industry (both mushrooms alone and mushroom soup) has greatly stimulated mushroom production.[27]

53. Are mushrooms grown outdoors superior to those grown indoors? Some people feel wild mushrooms have a better flavor than those grown inside. This is, of course, up to individual taste. One distinct disadvantage of wild mushrooms is their availability to mushroom flies, which lay their eggs in the gills. These eggs hatch to become grubs which eat their way through cap and stalk. Of course, another disadvantage is the possibility you will make a mistake in your identification. Commercial mushrooms have a much longer refrigerator life than wild mushrooms.

54. How long does it take for a mushroom to grow? The first commercial *(Agaricus)* mushrooms appear about 10 to 14 days after spawning. It then takes about 4 to 7 days to go from the pin head to harvest stages.[31] Maturity, not size, must be used to gauge the time of picking.[28] Wild Mushrooms: A few hours, days, weeks, seasons or years, depending upon the species.

55. **Why are mushrooms grown commercially in the dark while wild mushrooms develop without total darkness?** Remember, mushrooms are fungi which do not need light to make chlorophyll. Ordinary natural or artificial room light has no apparent effect on the growth of *Agaricus bisporus*. On the other hand sunlight shining on mushroom beds through window glass causes the compost to lose its moisture and cracks the mushroom caps. There are no electric lights over the mushroom beds because the beds or trays are arranged in such a way that light cannot get to them. It is more convenient and economical for the mushroom workers to wear a miner's helmet with its rechargeable, built-in light.

Some varieties of mushrooms do require light. All experiments with mushrooms have indicated that it is blue light that is needed and always at low levels. So it would generally be best to use north facing windows or fluorescent lamps.[13]

56. **Where can I find the location of the nearest mushroom farm?** When I tried to compile a list of mushroom farms to include in this book I was not successful. Most of the farms are located in southeastern Pennsylvania and nearby portions of Delaware and Maryland. Ralston Purina Co. recently entered the mushroom-growing business on a large scale. Their farms are in Zellwood, Florida; Morgan Hill, California; Madisonville, Texas; Princeton, Illinois; Loudon, Tennessee and Franklin, Connecticut. Moonlight Mushrooms are grown by Butler County Mushroom Farm, Inc. in exhausted limestone mines at West Winfield and Worthington, Pennsylvania.

Perhaps many farms don't advertise where they are located because the public tends to make a nuisance of themselves by being so curious about the eternally mysterious mushrooms.

57. **Why is spawn used for propagation rather than spores?** "The chief reason is that spores are unreliable. They germinate slowly, it is difficult to be certain that spores are genetically identical, and in most species, other than *Agaricus bisporus,* it is necessary to have fusion (anastomosis) of the mycelium of two spores before mycelium from spores will produce sporocarps (mushrooms). In the case of spawn, it is relatively easy to propagate only mycelium which has already anastomosed. Thus, the spawn serves to insure a better start for the culture and is more certain."[13]

58. **What are the future prospects for mushrooms?** Now that laboratories can prove the importance of mushrooms as an important food, mushroom sales are increasing yearly in industrialized nations.

Interestingly enough, mushrooms can be the answer to the protein deficiency of so many poor nations.

With some efforts mushroom production can be developed as a Cottage Industry in Asia since it does not require much land. Padi straw mushrooms grown in China and many other tropical countries in Southeast Asia, like Indonesia, the Philippines, Malaysia, Burma, etc., are perhaps the easiest and simplest in cultural requirements. The substratum is provided by the padi straw or wheat straw, which are abundantly available. The spawn preparation and spawning are also not specialized jobs as the old straw can be used for spawning of the new beds.[13]

The oyster mushroom is in commercial production in Europe. The species reportedly grown is *Pleurotus ostreatus.* In Japan and Taiwan several other species are cultivated. Work has also been done on the cultivation of the violet-spored oyster mushroom, *Pleurotus sapidus,* by Green Giant in the U. S. However, they are not pursuing it.[13]

Just because mushrooms can be grown and preserved, people will not necessarily eat them. For that reason it is necessary that the mushroom has acceptance among the population.[13]

59. How many commercial mushroom farms are there? In 1976 mushrooms were commercially grown by about 500 growers—about 30% fewer than a decade earlier. Although the number of growers has declined, the average size of operations per grower has expanded, and these operations have become more productive.[20] The structure of the mushroom industry is changing, as large agribusiness firms have been buying into the industry, or they are adding completely new production facilities as they branch out into this enterprise which is new to them.[12]

60. Is there an organization of mushroom businesses? Yes, smaller mushroom farms sometimes organize a local mushroom cooperative which serves as a sales outlet for them. The American Mushroom Institute is a national organization to help mushroom-oriented businesses.

61. How can I grow mushrooms? Many people seem to think growing mushrooms is an easy way to get rich quick. This is not possible. Mushroom growing is a well established and competitive field with a small margin of profit. According to the American Mushroom Institute it would cost approximately $50,000 to $70,000 to build a mushroom plant large enough to support one family. An additional $10,000 of working capital would be needed. To obtain profitable yields the grower not only needs buildings and equipment, he also needs a thorough knowledge of the principles of mushroom growing, plus experience.[12]

62. **What about mushroom growing at home as a hobby?** The cost of the material and labor for mushrooms produced at home may be greater than the cost of mushrooms purchased at the local store, however it is an interesting hobby. It is possible to purchase kits to grow *Agaricus* mushrooms from gift or seed catalogs.[12] Kits for *Agaricus bisporus,* Velvet stem *(Flammulina velutipes*—Winter Mushroom, *Enotake)*; Tree Oyster *(Pleuratus ostreatus)*; Wood Ears *(Auricularia polytrical)*; and Shiitake are available from The Kinoko Company, P. O. Box 6425, Oakland, Ca., 94621. These kits require only the last few steps of mushroom cultivation. They will mail you information upon your request.

There is a paperback book called *Growing Wild Mushrooms* by Bob Harris, (1976) Wingbow Press, Berkeley, Ca., $3.50, which describes how to make your own culture from wild mushrooms to grow on compost, inside. He makes an interesting statement, which I have never come across previously: "My experience with the fruiting of various mushrooms—both in cultures and with mushrooms in the wild—seems to readily follow the phases of the moon. The largest concentration being at or near the new moon until the full moon."

63. **How are mushrooms grown commercially?** Many people think of mushrooms growing in caves. Some do, but most come from groups of cement block or wooden, windowless, environmentally controlled buildings where they grow in trays or shelves.

A compost is made of a combination of carefully controlled materials which will be the food for the mushroom. The completed compost is put into the trays or shelves.

Spawn (seed) is planted in the compost where it spreads like cobwebs. One to two weeks later the compost is covered with a layer of sterile soil or peat about 1½ inches thick. This casing is kept lightly watered. The first mushrooms appear about five weeks after spawning. The room temperature is dropped to 58° to 62° F. Mushrooms continue to appear in 'flushes' every ten days for two or three months. The mushrooms are picked by twisting. The book *Mushroom Growing Today* by F. C. Atkins, Faber and Faber Limited or *Information on Mushroom Growing and The Mushroom Industry* by Aron Kinrus, available from American Mushroom Institute, P. O. Box 373, Kennett Square, Pa., 19348 ($2.50) will provide you with detailed information on the growing of mushrooms, but not how you can grow mushrooms.

64. **Can mushrooms be grown in a liquid medium (hydroponics)?** No, the presence of carbohydrates in the liquid stimulates the growth of airborne contaminating molds which soon crowd out the "mushroom mold."[16] However, Morel mushroom mycelium can be grown for food by the submerged culture process. (See Q102.)

65. **Where are most of the U. S. commercial mushrooms grown?** According to the U. S. Dept. of Agriculture Crop Reporting Board as of August 1977, figures showing state production:
    Pennsylvania (57%)   198,606,000 lbs.
    New York   8,072,000 lbs.
    Ohio   6,658,000 lbs.
    Delaware   7,027,000 lbs.
    Maryland   2,993,000 lbs.
    New Jersey   665,000 lbs.
Other states combined (Calif., Colo., Fla., Ga., Haw., Ill., Ind., Ky., Mass., Mich., Minn., Mo., Oreg., S. Dak., Tex., Utah, Va., Wash., and Wisc.)   123,108,000 lbs.[18]

66. **What do mushroom farms use to make the compost mushrooms use as food?** Mushrooms were originally grown using horse manure. When mushroom demand outgrew the horses' supply, synthetic recipes were developed which produced an even better, more dependable compost.

There are many compost recipes. Some of the ingredients used are horse or chicken manure, fish oils, brewers' grains, hay or straw, corn cobs, limestone, superphosphate, gypsum, dried blood, urea, soil.

Many growers in eastern Pennsylvania are using synthetic compost made according to a procedure developed cooperatively by Dr. J. W. Siden of the Pennsylvania State University, the Boy-Ar-Dee Mushroom Company at Milton, Pa., and the Butler Mushroom Company at West Winfield, Pa. The following is approximately the list of materials required for filling a double house: 15 tons of corn cobs, 7 tons of meadow hay, 4 tons of clover or alfalfa hay, ½ ton of gypsum, 500 pounds of ammonium nitrate, 500 pounds of muriate of potash, 1½ tons of dried brewers' grain or like amount of dried poultry manure, and a total of 10,000 to 11,000 gallons of water to give the desired moisture content.[16]

Composting is one of the trickiest parts of mushroom culture.[13] It takes 4 to 8 tons of compost to produce 1 ton of mushrooms.[28]

67. **How long does a mushroom planting produce mushrooms?** Approximately one-half of the yield is obtained within the first 30 days of harvest. After that the number and weight of mushrooms drops. The mushroom picking stage is 30-150 days although most commercial farms, for economic reasons, harvest only approximately 40 to 55 days. Then the compost is removed from the beds.[28]

68. **If I buy used compost from a mushroom farm, will mushrooms come up from it?** No, spent (used up) compost is usually pasteurized before it leaves the mushroom house. This kills any fungi it contains. Some mushroom farms reuse their compost, after a few

years, as casing, or as an ingredient in making new compost.[28]

69. **What is the best way I can use spent compost?** Nursery and garden mulch.[28]

70. **What does used compost cost?** Mushroom farms vary—where I purchase mine it costs $2.50 per ton, a regular pickup truck full costs about $3.00.

71. **What plant food value is left in the used compost?** Approximately 2% nitrogen on a basis of the dry weight of the compost.[28]

72. **How are mushrooms picked on commercial farms?** They are picked by hand. Picking machines have been patented but have not been successful on commercial farms. Picking is usually done by cutting the stems, but they may be pulled as well, and sometimes they will break off easily.[13]

73. **Are there any occupational diseases of mushroom workers?** Yes, some employees may develop Mushroom Worker's Lung, brought on by exposure to compost dust.[28]

74. **What is the average yield of mushrooms per square foot on a large commercial mushroom farm?** The average U. S. 1976-77 yield of *Agaricus bisporus* is 2.9 pounds per square foot per crop (shelf footage).[28] A different article said, "Current technology will allow over 125 pounds of mushrooms to be grown on a square foot of land every year (land footage). That is based upon five crops per year, trays or shelves stacked five high, and a yield of five pounds per square foot of bed per crop (Schroeder et al., 1974)."[14]

75. **Why don't farms turn on lights to pick mushrooms instead of using miners' helmets with lights?** Most commercial mushrooms grow in tiers of beds five beds high with narrow aisles between. Overhead lights are useless so each worker has his own light in the form of a miner's helmet which is battery powered.

76. **Do most mushroom farms have vistors' tours?** Due to insurance regulations most farms cannot allow non-employees beyond their offices.

77. **Are commercial mushrooms organically grown?** Chemicals are used against insects, mites and nematodes in thermal foggers. There was an article in the 1972 *Organic Farming* magazine telling of a grower in California who had stopped all spraying and had become a Certified Organic mushroom grower. I wrote to him asking about his operation but he never replied.

Mushrooms are subject to the same rules and regulations as any farm crop. State agricultural requirements and controls are established and followed concerning pesticides. Detailed information on pests and chemical control can be found in *Mushroom Growing and The Mushroom Industry.* (See Q131.)

78. **If there is only one U. S. commercially grown mushroom, how can there be so many strains of it?** Strains can be altered by subjecting the spores to mutant-producing agencies such as ultra-violet radiation and salts of radio-active elements such as uranium and cobalt.[4]

CONSUMPTION

79. **What percent of U. S. mushrooms are sold fresh and processed?**

MUSHROOMS: Sales by Type and Percent of Total, 1966-77

Year	Fresh Market Volume of Sales	Percent	Processing Volume of Sales	Percent	Total Production
1966-67	41,951	25	122,964	75	164,915
1967-68	47,611	26	132,980	74	180,591
1968-69	56,024	30	132,783	70	188,807
1969-70	62,115	32	131,764	68	193,879
1970-71	58,269	28	148,541	72	206,810
1971-72	66,323	29	165,050	71	231,373
1972-73	76,728	30	177,274	70	254,002
1973-74	102,293	37	177,200	63	279,493
1974-75	126,118	42	172,963	58	299,081
1975-76	142,121	46	167,695	54	309,816
1976-77	151,247	44	195,882	56	347,129

from USDA Crop Reporting Board Aug. 12, 1977.

80. **Why are people buying more fresh mushrooms?**
    1. Increased availability of fresh mushrooms in many areas of the U. S., resulting from the location of new growing facilities closer to nontraditional markets, and promotional work by the American Mushroom Institute, the Mushroom Canners Committee, and others;
    2. Increased availability of fresh mushrooms during the summer months;
    3. An increase in per capita disposable income;
    4. An increase in the U. S. population;
    5. The growing popularity of mushrooms among weight conscious consumers;
    6. Prices, which until very recently were increasing much more slowly than the prices of most other categories of fresh and processed vegetables.

Also it is generally acknowledged in the mushroom industry that the botulism scare of 1973/74 affected consumer confidence in canned mushroom products.[20]

81. **What were the facts behind the botulism problems with mushrooms?** Webster's definition of botulin: "a toxin that is formed by the botulinus and is the direct cause of botulism." Webster's defini-

tion of botulism: "acute food poisoning caused by botulin in food."

On April 5, 1973, following disclosure of the third instance in 1973 of the finding of the bacterium Clostridium botulinum in domestically processed mushrooms, the U. S. Food and Drug Administration announced plans to investigate the domestic mushroom processing industry. As a result of this investigation, Clostridium botulinum spores and/or toxin were found to be present in the canned mushroom product of several firms. FDA recommendations and requirements for appropriate corrective measures were made. Included were procedures for precise record keeping of such critical functions as cooking time, filled weight, and can seam examinations. To survey mushrooms produced prior to the corrective program, FDA made visual examinations of warehouse stocks, followed by laboratory analysis of suspected products. Visual examination is a reliable inspection tool because cans containing the botulinum toxin would virtually always be swollen or leaking or otherwise abnormal. Recalls eventually affected 10 firms, 8 domestic and 2 foreign.[19]

82. **How many mushroom canneries are there in the U. S.?** In the 1975-76 marketing year mushrooms were canned by 29 firms, compared with 35 in 1972. About half of the canners are in Pennsylvania, most of the other firms are in California, Ohio, Michigan and Washington. Three groups of primary suppliers market canned mushrooms in the U. S.
  1. Canners, which market only the domestically produced product.
  2. Canner-importers, which market both the domestic and the foreign products.
  3. Importers, which market only the foreign produced product.
In 1975-76, both canners and importers sold the largest share of their products directly to institutional outlets.[20]

83. **Do mushroom imports hurt our mushroom industry?** There is a big debate going on about this question. Canned mushroom imports *(Agaricus bisporus)* on a fresh weight basis, increased irregularly from 5 million pounds in marketing year 1960-61 to 88 million pounds in 1975-76.

In September, 1975, the Mushroom Processors Association and the Mushroom Processors Tariff Committee filed a petition with the U. S. International Trade Commission for import relief.[19] Two investigations resulted.[20] The findings are published in U. S. International Trade Commission Publications 761-March, 1976 and 798-January, 1977. Chairman (1977) Daniel Minchew's view was: There were several factors which may have led to any decline that the domestic (canning) industry may have suffered. He considers three of these factors, moreover, to be important: (1) increased imports, (2) the increasing diversion of fresh mushrooms' production to the fresh market and to processors other than canners, (3) the discovery of *Clostridium botulinum* and/or botulinal toxin (botulism) in canned mushrooms in 1973.[20]

He has concluded again in this investigation that botulism food poisoning (1973-74) is a more important factor than increased imports in any "serious injury" that the domestic industry may have suffered.[20]

84. **What are the U. S. mushroom producers doing to compete with imports?** They are relying heavily upon Penn State University to develop and test more efficient mushroom growing, processing, and marketing techniques. The general trend in mushroom engineering has been toward the development of mechanical equipment to reduce labor costs and to provide better environmental control.

The Penn State Horticulture Department has recently (1975) developed a means of improving quality and reducing mushroom shrinkage during canning (treating mushrooms in a vacuum chamber).

The American Mushroom Institute (AMI) has served to unite the growers in a program of cooperative advertising and self-improvement through educational programs. They have worked closely with food editors in developing new mushroom recipes, conducted educational programs to encourage wider use of mushrooms, and provided other useful information for their members and consumers. Domestic canners have tried to become more competitive by increasing the production of the less labor-intensive stems-and-pieces style of pack, while decreasing production of the whole, buttons, and sliced styles of pack.[20]

85. **What countries are the principal suppliers of canned mushrooms?** Marketing year (July 1—June 30) U. S. Imports by pounds 1975-76:

Republic of China (Taiwan)	36,050,000
Republic of Korea	18,009,000
Japan	1,227,000
Costa Rica	189,000
France	419,000
Dominican Republic	661,000
All others	799,000
Total	57,351,000

Source: Compiled from official statistics of the U. S. Dept. of Commerce.[20]

The principal importers are: The Federal Republic of Germany (West Germany), the U. S., and Canada, in that order. Other importers of significance are: Australia, Japan, Sweden, and Switzerland.[20]

WILD MUSHROOMS

86. **What is the best way to learn about wild mushrooms?** Purchase or borrow a good illustrated identification book. A small size is easier to carry with you. From it learn the right times and places to look for mushrooms. Inquire around for a person to help you learn.

Check with local colleges for available classes.

Become a member of a mycological society. Through them you may find a club in your area.

87. **How do I join a mycological society?** Nationally there are two of them. One is the North American Mycology Association, 3 Ginger Hill Lane, Toledo, Ohio, 43623, which is easier for amateurs to understand.

Their literature reads as follows: "Active membership (includes family) $6.00 and student membership $2.00. WHAT NAMA IS: The North American Mycological Assoc. is a nonprofit corporation founded in 1961 for the following purposes: To provide a meeting ground for all persons interested in mushrooms. Stimulate public interest in mushrooms. Aid those who wish to increase their knowledge about mushrooms and promote scientific study of fungi.

"WHAT NAMA DOES: Publishes six issues per year of the newsletter *Nycophile* which gives mycological news, wide-ranging information, notice of events of interest to members, reviews of recent books and poison information. Publishes the journal *McIlvainea* containing keys and articles by the world's leading taxonomists and mycologists. Holds annual forays in the finest collecting areas in the country, often with short courses in mycology, always with lectures by professionals. In 1975 held an international exhibit of drawings of fungi and a European foray in four countries.

"Conducts a Round Robin Slide Exchange, an annual photo contest, and loans slide sets of the winning slides of each contest.

"WHAT NAMA CAN DO FOR YOU: Increase your knowledge of mushrooms. Keep you informed about activities in this field. Put you in touch with people who have a similar interest in mycology, whether it is taxonomy, habitat, toxicity or edibility."

The Mycological Society of America, Office of the Secretary-Treasurer, Department of Botany, University of Florida, Gainsville, Florida, 32611, is aimed more toward professional mycologists.

Information on their application card reads as follows: "Any person interested in the study of fungi is eligible for membership. Annual dues of Regular Members are $15.00. A special annual rate of $8.00, for a maximum of 5 years, is provided for a member enrolled as a student. Regular and student members receive *Mycologia,* the *MSA Newsletter* and a worldwide membership list. Membership may begin either on January 1 of the current year or the next January 1."

88. **Where can I get information about wild mushrooms growing in my area?** Telephone your County Court House and ask for the extension service office. Then ask if they have Extension Bulletins on mushrooms.

For example Michigan has 5 excellent bulletins illustrated in color published by the Cooperative Extension Service of Michigan State University: 1. *May is Morel Month in Michigan,* Ext. Bulletin E-614, 21 pages, 25¢; 2. *Mushrooms Grow on Stumps,* Ext. Bulletin E-924, 32 pages, 75¢; 3. *Wood Waste Makes Wonderful Mushrooms,* Ext. Bulletin E-925, 21 pages, 60¢; 4. *Best of The Boletes,* Ext. Bulletin E-926, 22 pages, 60¢; 5. *Don't Pick Poison!,* 49 pages, 75¢. (To order send money with order to Michigan State University Bulletin Office, P. O. Box 231, East Lansing, Michigan 48824.)

Indiana, Missouri and Minnesota all have the same bulletin, *Edible Wild Mushrooms,* B-357, 25¢ each.

The Mushroom Hunter's Field Guide by Alexander H. Smith, published by The University of Michigan, 1963, is useful throughout the United States and Canada.

89. **How can I identify a mushroom?** (The following is from *Mushrooms Grow on Stumps,* Michigan State Ext. Bulletin E-924, by Ingrid Bartelli)

"Until it becomes routine practice, study a mushroom in this manner:

1. Look at the top or cap

Is the surface smooth, rough, wrinkled, hairy, scaly, moist, sticky, slimy, dry, watermarked?

What shape is it when young in the button stage, when mature and in old speciments?

What color is it at all stages of growth?

Is the margin of the cap even, broken, lobed, wavy, incurved, uplifted, marked with striations, pock marked?

Is the cap attached securely to the stalk or does it lift off easily?

2. Then look under the cap

First observe the color in young as compared to older specimens.

What is the nature of the spore-producing surface (gills, spines, pores, tubes)?

Is there evidence of any tissue (veil) covering the underside of the cap in young specimens? It is attached to the stalk and to the edge of the cap.

If so, how does it rupture when the cap expands? Does the tissue stick to the stalk, forming a ring or annulus on the stalk? Do parts of the veil tissue tear off and adhere to the margin of the cap?

3. In case of a gilled mushroom, are the gills crowded or far apart (distant)?

How are the gills attached to the stalk? Are they notched, squarely attached? Do they run down the stalk? Or are they completely free of the stalk?

Are the edges of the gills broken, jagged like a saw, even, wavy? Are the gills all the same length or are there short ones interspersed between the entire ones? Do gills fork? Are there veins between them?

4. Then study the stalk

Observe its size, shape, surface, color and texture. Is it hollow, stuffed, cartilaginous, fibrous, solid?

Does it have an annulus or ring? What is at the base of the stalk? A cup, bulb? How far below the surface of the soil must you dig to find the entire base of the mushroom?

The color of the spores or 'seeds' is critical for identification. The color of the mushroom spores is always the same for a single species, but varies from white through the color spectrum for different species. A spore print will tell you their color."[7]

The North American Mycology Assoc. sends its members ISCC-NBS Centroid Color Charts based on the Muncell system of color designation which is most widely used in schools throughout North America. There are 267 color blocks to use for universal color identification.

Even using all the above study guides you may not be able to determine the right identification. Specialists, at times, have to resort to microscopic study for positive identification.

Never become overconfident of your mushroom identification skills.

90. **How do I make a spore print?** Cut off the cap at the top of the stalk. Place the cap, gills down, on white paper for dark gills, dark colored paper for white gills. Spore prints are best when the mushroom is protected from air currents which might move the spores and dry out the cap so use a bowl or box to cover them.

If the cap is too young the spores have not yet developed, if too old the spores may have already blown away.

91. **How are mushrooms labeled for mycological collection?** (Some people are mushroom searchers like others are bird watchers, taking notes of the species they locate, etc. It's lots of fun!) Label each species (picture, drawing or dried specimen), date of collection, place

of collection, color, size, odor, substrate (what it was growing on), habit of growth, any other descriptive feature, and spore print.

92. **Why does a mushroom species vary in shape or color?** The source of their food, the chemicals in the air, the altitude and latitude all affect the color, shape, and flavor of mushrooms.

93. **What are the recommended edible wild mushrooms for beginners to look for?** Professor Clyde M. Christensen of the University of Minnesota suggests beginners limit themselves to 4 of the nearly 50 species of common edible wild mushrooms. These 4 are safe and easy to identify: 1. Morel; 2. Puffball; 3. Shaggy Mane; 4. Sulphur polypore *(Polypours sulphureus)*. Be sure to use a good illustrated mushroom handbook for identification. Cooking instructions are in recipe section.

An excellent cookbook *Wild Mushroom Recipes* by the Puget Sound Mycological Society is available from Pacific Search Press, 715 Harrison street, Seattle, Washington, 98109 for $6.95 plus 75¢ postage and handling (Washington State residents must include sales tax.) It has over 200 wild mushroom recipes.

94. **What can I do to protect myself when eating wild mushrooms?** I will answer this with a quote from *The Mushroom Hunter's Field Guide* by Alexander H. Smith, Profesor Emeritus, University of Michigan, "Some fungi are poisonous to some people but not to others." Keeping this in mind:

"1. Eat only one kind at a time so that if any difficulty should develop the cause is known.

2. Eat only young or freshly matured specimens free from insect larvae (worms).

3. Cook the specimens well.

4. Eat only small amounts when testing a species you have not tried previously.

5. Do not overindulge under any circumstances. There is always danger of indigestion from eating too much of any food.

6. Have each member of the family test each new kind for himself or herself. The most important precaution, however, is to be critical of your specimens and make sure you have them correctly identified."[30]

Do not pick mushrooms which have been frozen in cold weather.

Do not pick mushrooms which have been in the rain for many days. Even if they look good they will be tasteless.

95. **How do I keep in good condition the mushrooms I am picking?** Gather them in a shallow, rigid container. A box or basket with handles is the most convenient. Keep them away from the sun in a cool, well-ventilated place. Pick only the fresh mushrooms in a group, especially if you are transporting them a long distance. Never use plastic bags for collecting or storage. The weight of mushrooms piled upon one another will crush them. Storing mushrooms in bags, tubs or anything deep will also lead to a collection of moisture from respiration and condensation.

Consider the temperature of your car trunk before you store mushrooms inside. If they are inside the car be sure the sun is not shining through the glass onto them.

96. **How long can you keep wild mushrooms?** Generally speaking, fungi for food should be gathered while they are still young and unblemished and they should be eaten within six hours. If that is not possible then they should be boiled in slightly salted water, drained and stored in the refrigerator where they will keep for 24 hours or so.

Wild mushrooms do not disintegrate or go mushy when boiled and in many instances the flavor is improved by long slow cooking which tends to make a more tasty dish than a quick over-hot session in the frying pan.[29]

97. **Are there ways to force worms and bugs to leave mushrooms?** *The Complete Book of Mushrooms* says to place picked mushrooms in the gathering basket with stalks turned up. They claim this will start the worms moving toward the base of the stalk so you can get rid of them.[26]

For years people have soaked mushrooms in salt water to drive out the live things. Of course, it also drives out the mushroom flavor.

98. **Why do safe edible mushrooms make some people sick?** The decay organisms in rotting mushrooms have been known to poison people even though the mushrooms were safe when fresh.

People who are allergic to strawberries, tomatoes, shellfish, etc., may also be allergic to mushrooms.

Young children and the elderly may also have bad reactions to the mushroom proteins.

People sometimes eat too many at a time or too many close together.

99. **Why are wild mushrooms so hard to find one year and plentiful the next?** The temperature and moisture determine wild mushroom growth.

100. **If I pick all the mushrooms in an area will that stop them**

from coming up there again? "Picking the mushrooms, as far as future crops are concerned, has no more effect on the mushroom plant than picking the apples from a tree. It is impossible to strip an area of any of its mushrooms by gathering the fruits. As pointed out, the survival of a given patch of spawn is determined by the food supply, and new spawn is not likely to establish itself in an area in which the food supply has already been exhausted by an older spawn of the same species."[30]

101. **What is a fairy ring?** Rings start from an original clump, spreading outward each year as they search for food. Either the food was used up in the center so no mushrooms grew there or the threads of the fungus blocked all the air spaces between the soil particles so rain water could not soak in causing other vegetation to die. Eventually the mycelium dries up and vegetation returns on the inside of the ring.

Some fairy rings have been slowly expanding for hundreds of years. Sometimes the circle is broken by a building or stream. Some rings are estimated to be 400 years old.

Aerial photographs show them more easily than they can be located on the ground.

Often the grass outside the circle is greener than inside it showing how the mushrooms have depleted the nutrients.

Before the microscope when people did not understand how mushrooms grew they explained a mysterious circle of mushrooms as a place where fairies (or witches) had danced during the night and the mushrooms appeared where their feet touched the ground. The French name for them is rond de sorcieres and the German is hexenring.

102. **Are morel (*Morchella esculenta*) mushrooms grown commercially?** No, the spawn grows well in culture, but does not fruit . . . However, United States patent #3,086,320, April 23, 1963, was issued to cover the production of the myceliae by the submerged culture process (in liquid).

The myceliae pellets were fully grown in the form of balls, ¼ to 1 inch in diameter in 10 to 13 days, then were dried and powdered.[22] The Company which obtained the patent no longer grows them. I could not find out why.

103. **Is it safe to eat any kind of morel (spongy looking) mushroom?** No, there are kinds of false morels. *Verpa bohemica*, *Gyromitra esculenta* and *Gyromitra infula* are examples. (See Q123.)

104. **What is the difference between the true and false morel?** The false morels have a wrinkled instead of a pitted head. Refer to a mushroom identification book for illustrations of varieties.

105. **Is it against the law to sell wild mushrooms for food?** Most states have laws regarding the sale of wild mushrooms for human consumption. The authority is usually vested in the state department of health or the state food inspection department.

In some states there is no specific regulation concerning mushrooms but they would be covered under such a law as Michigan's which says that any food sold for human consumption must be wholesome and of a variety that is known to be safe. The responsibility for quality of a food product is upon the seller.[5]

In some foreign countries where wild mushrooms are sold on the open market, much like our farmers' markets, the ministry of health determines which species of mushrooms can be sold. As many as 50 or 60 different species are permissible for sale in some countries. Inspectors are hired to see that the mushrooms are actually those on the label.[5]

106. **Is it possible to grow my own wild mushrooms?** Oyster mushrooms can be cultivated on newly cut stumps, and some people water a good stump to encourage mushroom production. To grow puffballs, break open a dry and powdery puffball into a bag and mix in some dried animal manure. Scatter it in various locations in your yard or fields. Sprinkle ⅛" of dirt over the seeded places and pack down lightly. (See Q62.)

107. **Why was the *Agaricus bisporus* chosen to be the common commercial mushroom of the west?** Explanation given by Dr. R. H. Kurtzman, Jr., Western Regional Research Service, U. S. Dept. of Agriculture: "All domesticated plants came from wild species, although many have undergone extensive breeding. Why the *Agaricus bisporus* was ever chosen seems to be a great mystery, but most authors seem to ascribe its cultivation to an unfortunate mistake or mutation. They believe that man intended to cultivate the common meadow mushroom, *Agaricus campestrius,* which is held in much higher esteem by connoisseurs."[13]

108. **Is there a list of the best tasting wild mushrooms?** I came across one called *"Gastronomic Classification of Mushrooms"* in the *Complete Book of Mushrooms* (see Bibliography) prepared by an expert mycologist and experienced collector who has personally tested the edibility of more than six hundred species of mushrooms. They are divided into four groups: first, second, third and fourth quality. He also included a few wild mushrooms which can be eaten raw.[26] If you are a serious mushroom student this book would be a great addition to your library (price $17.95).

109. **Is it true that fox fire is really mushrooms?** Yes, it is the

spawn of the mushroom fungus *Armillaria mellea* (edible) that causes decaying wood to glow.

Wood infested with this mycelium will glow as long as it is damp and the mycelium is alive. The fruit of this mushroom (also known as honey mushrooms) does not produce any light.

The Jack O'Lantern, *Omphalotus illudens,* (sometimes called *Clitocybe illudens*—poisonous), occasionally gives off such a strong light you can find them in the dark.

Fungus light varies from white, through yellowish-green to blue-green. The strength of the light depends upon the temperature. The glow is probably caused by luciferin which is also found in glow worms.[29]

110. **Since most mushroom ideification books talk about mycorrhizal relationships, just what is a mycorrhiza?** This awkward word means "fungus root" (myco, fungus, and rhiza, root, adapted from the Greek). A peculiar kind of root formed by the white threads of a fungus encloses a tree root with a heavy, white hairy mantle. The result is a stubby thick root which looks like a deformity but is actually an efficient root organ that contributes to the health of the tree.[23]

111. **How does mycorrhizal growth differ from destructive attacks of fungi?** The threads of the fungus seem to be more efficient than root hairs in imbibing both mineral salts and organic nitrogen from the ground. In return for this service, the tree has only to pay with its sugar, which the leaves manufacture so abundantly that there is plenty to spare. Moreover, the fungus does not poison roots or inhibit root hairs. It adds a larger and longer-lasting organ of nourishment-collecting to the normal complement of root hairs.

When A. B. Frank, Professor of Plant Physiology in Berlin, concluded that the mycorrhiza represents a cooperation between mushroom and tree which helps both, and is not the attack of a parasite, a storm of protest arose. This kind of root looks diseased, but the trees on which it is found are the healthiest. Much research has confirmed the early theory. Today soil is inoculated with the mushrooms to improve the crops of trees, as well as many other crops. It is said that the flourishing Southern yellow pines depend on mycorrhiza for their existence.[23]

112. **What kind of fungi form mycorrhizas with trees?** They are the everyday mushrooms of the woodland.[23]

113. **Does each kind of tree prefer a certain kind of mushroom?** Trees have preferences. Birch often uses the fly amanita; white pine likes the milky mushroom *(Lactarius);* Scotch pine prefers boletus;

beech and oak seem to prefer a puffball. But there is no positive way in which trees and mushrooms choose partners. Some mushrooms will be found on a number of different trees.[23]

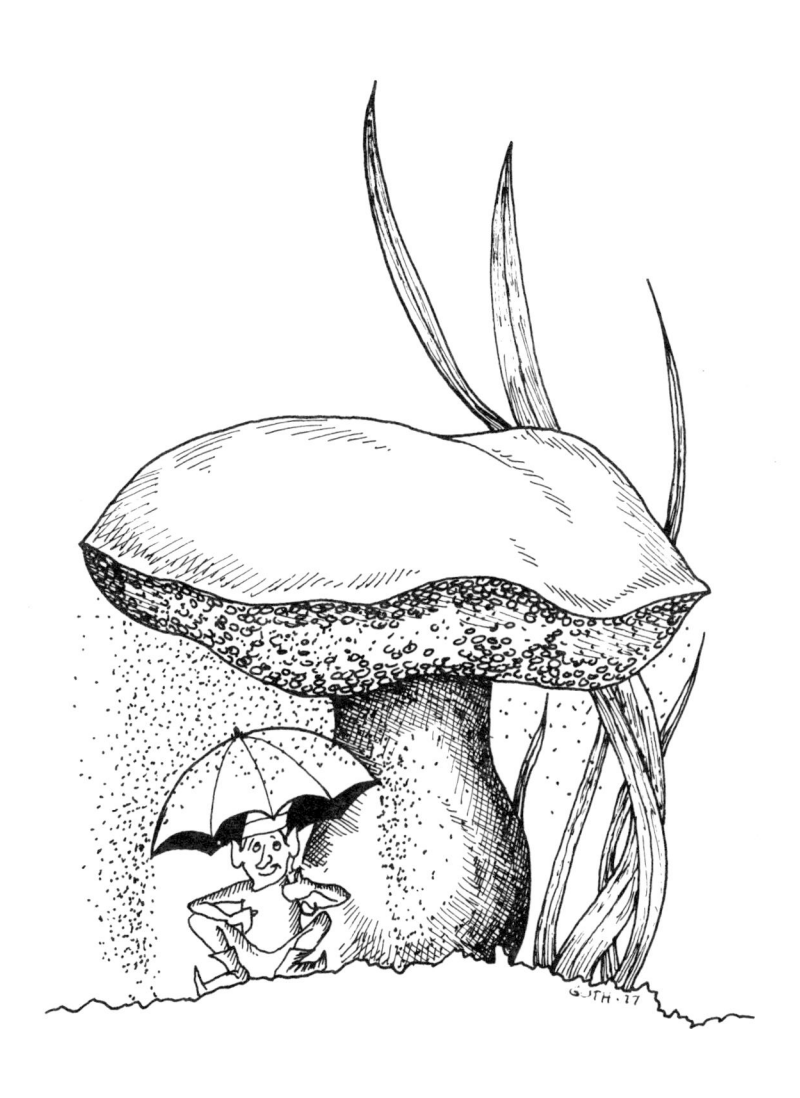

POISONOUS

114. **Can I get poisoned by touching a poisonous mushroom (like poison ivy)?** No, you have to eat or inhale the mushroom's poison.

115. **How can a person tell which mushrooms are poisonous?** Use a book as a guide to positive identification. Don't eat any wild mushrooms unless you can identify them with one hundred percent certainty.

The use of continually improved, sophisticated instruments and equipment by dedicated, eminent scientists is resulting in greatly increased knowledge in the field of mushroom toxins.[5]

116. **Are there tests to prove that a mushroom is safe to eat?** There are no simple tests you can use to prove mushrooms are safe or poisonous. POSITIVE IDENTIFICATION IS YOUR ONLY PROTECTION IN EATING WILD MUSHROOMS.

117. **Why are people poisoned?** (from *Don't Pick Poison!* See Q88.)

1. Because of innocence or ignorance—they don't realize there are poisonous mushrooms so they eat any of them.

2. Some eat too much at one time or repeatedly at successive meals—toxins build up and accumulate in the body to the "unsafe" limits.

3. Mistaken identity—it is easy to mistake the identity of a mushroom since so many look alike.

4. Carelessness, especially in years of heavy fruitings.

5. Picking at a time when it is hard to identify a mushroom: when it's too dark to see detail clearly; in the rain or soon after when mushrooms are wet, or perhaps when the senses of observation are dulled by fatigue or by alcohol.

6. It is easy to make a mistake in identity if you collect mushrooms in the button stage. How many wild flowers could you identify from the bud alone?

7. The cases of mushroom poisoning among young children often result from the developmental fact that a child learns about his world by trying to eat everything he can get to his mouth. The fact that the mushrooms are eaten raw adds to the hazard.

8. Some accidents have been caused because the victim had to perform—to show off. "See this mushroom! It's good to eat. I'll prove it to you!"

9. Wild mushrooms, even some considered edible, have caused distress when eaten by persons who tend to be allergic to various foods, pollens, etc., or are in poor health.

10. Some accidents happen to folks whose minds are geared to their stomachs. They live to eat. Just the sheer beauty of some wild mushrooms makes them look "good enough to eat."

11. A surprising number of persons insist on experimenting, using themselves as guinea pigs. This is more apt to be true among the young and adventurous, often seeking some mind-affecting or intoxicating results. They'll often continue their "experiments" until they suffer some poisonous effect.

118. **What are the symptoms of mushroom poisoning?** Poisoning can show up in the following ways:

1. Mild allergy—similar to reactions from eating strawberries or shellfish, sometimes caused by eating too many in a short time. (Some people react this way to commercial mushrooms.)

2. Ebriety (drunk type reaction)—hallucinations, perhaps short coma.

3. Severe gastrointestinal disturbance—lack of muscular coordination, vomiting, diarrhea, stomach pain.

4. Fatal—vomiting, diarrhea, heavy perspiration, thirst, cold hands and feet, finally paralysis and convulsions. This agony can last for 10 to 20 days. The poison destroys the liver and kidneys, causes heart failure and internal bleeding. Doctors are able to save some strong bodied people but their bodies are permanently damaged.

Causes of these symptoms are:

1. Real poisonous mushrooms.

2. Wild mushrooms which have become poisonous as a result of frost or old age (ptomaine poisoning).

3. Drinking alcohol during or after eating *Coprinus atramentarius* (inky caps).

4. Body reactions to safe mushrooms (allergies).

119. **What symptoms might you have when you mix alcohol and inky caps?** Symptoms are initiated early after combining alcohol and *Coprinus atramentarius* or by the consumption of alcohol up to 48 hours after eating this mushroom. Intense flushing of the face and neck, a metallic taste in the mouth, heart pounding and a feeling of swollen hands are the early symptoms. Nausea, vomiting and a state of confusion generally follow. *C. atramentarius* contains a chemical compound that interferes with the metabolism of alcohol, causing

acetaldehyde to accumulate in the blood. The dramatic reactions cease with time and reassurance. They may last as long as eight hours. (5) Some people may have problems even drinking tea or coffee while or after eating these particular mushrooms.[26]

120. **What should a person do if they think they may have eaten a poisonous mushroom?** Call a doctor. Find out exactly what kind of mushroom was eaten, if at all possible. Were there parts left after cleaning it or in the vomit? Save these. Induce vomiting only if mushrooms have been recently eaten. If more than 8-10 hours have passed since eating the mushrooms they have entered into the intestine. Go to a hospital immediately.

When you cook a batch of wild mushrooms make it a habit to put an uncooked few into the refrigerator in case you need to reidentify them.

The U. S. Dept. of Agriculture has established a Poison Fungi Center in Beltsville, Maryland, which will be a reporting station and clearing house for cases of mushroom poisoning.

121. **How do scientists know which mushrooms are poisonous?** "Various poisonous species have different active chemicals, and hence produce different symptoms. On the other hand there are groups of species with the same general types of poisons."[30]

"Through the years our knowledge of poisonous species has been built up through case histories of people who thought they were eating an edible species but got sick enough to need a doctor. Since different people react differently to certain species, it is readily understood why it is not practical to test species on a laboratory animal and make general recommendations as to the edibility from such tests. The reason for many apparent contradictions in the literature on poisonous mushrooms is also apparent. By the time a doctor has been called to a case it is often almost impossible to learn the identity of the fungus which actually caused the trouble."[30]

122. **Which mushrooms have the mind-altering drug?** Some of them are the *Aminta muscarie* (Fly Agaric), *Psilocybe semilanceata, Psilocybe cyanescens, Panaeolus subbalteatus* and *Psilocybe pugetensis.*

123. **Which are the most deadly mushrooms?** About 95% of reported mushroom fatalities have been caused by eating mushrooms from the genus (group) called *Amanita* or from the genus called *Galerina.* People may not realize they have been poisoned until 10 or 12 or more hours after they have eaten the mushrooms. Death usually follows in three to seven days.[5] The lethal dose for a man of medium size is 20 grams (less than one ounce).[26]

The *Amanita phalloides* (Death Cap) button stage looks like and grows beside the *Agaricus campestris,* the wild species of the commercial *Agaricus bisporus.* This is why the *Agaricus* is not one of the recommended mushrooms for beginners to collect for eating.

The *Amanita* can be identified by the cup (volva) at the base of the stem (stipe). The *Agaricus capestris* does not have this cup.

The Pasteur Institute in France makes a serum to help save a poisoned person's life but no antidote is known.[29] In very recent years, some U. S. lives have been saved by a thioctic acid treatment used in Czechoslovakia.[5]

At least seven deaths in North America have been attributed to poisoning from *Gyromitra esculenta* or *Gyromitra infula* (false morels) commonly called the beefsteak, elephant ears or the brain mushroom. They contain the poison monomethylhydrazine.[6]

Monomethylhydrazine (often used in rocket fuel) affects the nervous system, with damage to liver, blood and kidneys.

Thousands of people eat *Gyromitra esculenta* deliberately. They get by with it because monomethylhydrazine is volatile—it evaporates when heated—and because liquid in which the mushrooms are cooked is discarded. Apparently humans have some tolerance to the poison, and only when it is consumed in large quantities or repeatedly does it trigger the symptoms of *Gyromitra* poisoning. It is suspected, however, that even though one does not experience the poisoning symptoms, some damage to kidneys, blood and liver does occur.[5]

124. **Are there any specialized books on mushroom poisoning?**
Yes . . . coming out in 1977 . . . *Toxic and Hallucinogenic Mushroom Poisoning: A Handbook for Physicians and Mushroom Hunters* by G. Lincoff and D. H. Mitchel available from Van Nostrand Reinhold Co., New York; Michigan State University Bulletin *Don't Pick Poison.* (See Q88.) A technical publication on poisonous mushrooms is to be released by the U. S. Dept. of Agricultre in 1977. *California Toxic Fungi* by Dr. Thomas J. Duffy and Paul P. Vergeer, 34 pp., 10 color plates, 3 figures plus a toxin chart. Price $3.50. The booklet covers the seven recognized toxin groups. Perhaps the outstanding feature of the text is a chart listing 117 species placed in their proper toxin group. The North American Mycological Association recommends it to all mycophagists in America. It will be of particular value to physicians because it explains clearly the symptoms and varied methods of treatment according to the type of toxin ingested. Most of the species mentioned also occur in other areas of the United States and Europe, and this booklet will therefore be of general value. Order from: Mycological Society of San Francisco, Inc., P. O. Box 904, San Francisco, California 94101. *Hallucinogenic & Poisonous Mushroom Field Guide,* by Gary P. Menser, And/Or Press, Berkeley, California, 160 pp., 39 color plates, 50 line drawings with keys and charts, price $5.95. Order from And/Or Press, Box 2246, Berkeley, California 94702.

MISCELLANEOUS

125. Why do many foreign people (or their children) especially appreciate mushrooms as food? Religious customs have often had an important effect on the eating habits of nations and in those areas of Eastern Europe where the Greek Orthodox Church decreed periods of fasting in pre-Communist days, fungi assumed an added importance in places where fish was not always easily obtainable. This is one of the reasons why in Russia and the countries adjoining, fungi have been used more widely than anywhere else and many ways of cooking them have been devised.[29]

Primitive tribes in other parts of the world also rely to a great extent on fungi. During wars and famines fungus eating has saved the lives of a great many people in Europe who would otherwise have starved to death.[29]

Nearly 300 different kinds of mushrooms are sold in markets in Sweden. In Finland, Poland and Russia the Lactarius species is very popular. European and Scandinavian descendants in America and Canada still have mushroom knowledge.[29]

126. What are the religious superstitutions about mushrooms? The answers printed here are from the book *The Sacred Mushroom and The Cross* by John M. Allegro.

Before the invention of the microscope people believed that fungi were one of the greatest of the marvels of nature since they belonged to a class of things that sprang up spontaneously and could not be grown from seed and lived without a root. Some people thought fertilization was done by thunder since mushrooms rapidly appeared after thunderstorms, then rapidly disappeared. Since they thought God spoke through thunder, mushrooms were considered "Sons of God." The sacred fungus became known as "the Holy Plant" throughout the ancient world.

Every aspect of the mushroom's existence was fraught with sexual allusions. It was, they felt, God himself, manifest on earth. To the mystic it was the divinely given means of entering heaven.

The strange shapes and manner of growth of the fungus, along with its poisonous reputation, combined to evoke feelings of awe and dread in the mind of simple folk.

The mushroom became the centre of a mystery cult in the Near East which persisted for thousands of years. There seems good evidence it swept from there into India in the cult of the Soma some 3,500 years ago; it certainly flourished in Siberia until quite recent times, and is found even today in certain parts of South America.

Thus the extraordinary situation has arisen that this most important mushroom cult, from which much of the mythology of the ancient Near East sprang, has been almost completely overlooked by the historians. In the Bible "mushroom" has been nowhere noted although one of its most ancient names, Hebrew *Kotereth,* Accadian *Katarru* appears many times in its straightforward meaning of "mushroom-shaped" capital of a pillar (1 Kgs 7:16, etc).[2]

127. **Have you heard of the mushroom artists use to draw on?** Its name is *Ganoderma applanatum.* It is generally fan-shaped and grows horizontal to the ground on dead and rotting hardwood trees or stumps. It ranges from an inch to 12 to 14 inches across.

The fungus has a tough, woodlike upper surface and a soft, white, velvety underside. It is the lower side that is used to draw on.

They should be gathered in the fall. Use a small ax or hatchet to separate the mushroom from the stump without touching the white underside since fingerprints can ruin it. If you try collecting and drawing in the spring or summer the fungus heals over and your picture disappears.

Scratch in your artwork within a hour or two for a brown and white pen and ink type drawing or let the mushroom dry and carve it instead.

If holes appear from boring type bugs inside, lightly spray with an aerosol bug killer.

128. **Are there mushroom research laboratories?** Yes, *Agaricus bisporus,* the mushroom strain grown commercially, has been the subject of research by Penn State University, University of Texas and Massachusetts State College. Private companies such as the Campbell Soup Co., Brandywine Corp., Mushroom Supply Co., Grocery Store Products Co., American Mushroom Corp., and the Butler County Mushroom Co. have their own research facilities. The USDA also conducts mushroom research in their Western Regional Laboratory at Berkeley, Ca. and at their Agricultural Research Center in Beltsville, Md.

129. **What are some of the results of mushroom research?** The mushroom industry has benefitted tremendously from the research done at Penn State University. In the 1930's Dr. James Sinden found a reliable way to grow mycelium on specially prepared grain (instead of compost) to produce a spawn free of disease or mold. The college obtained patents on it in 1932 and 1933. The proceeds from the royalties, about $250,000, provided a sizeable budget to support the University's total research program. Dr. Sinden also found a way to shorten the composting cycle and to produce a compost from hay, corn cobs and other materials.

Penn State is continually working on the mushroom shrinkage problem, compost formulas, development of more productive strains of mushrooms, production technology, disease and insect control.

Their mushroom research and extension staff are from the following departments: Plant Pathology; Entomology; Food Science; Agricultural Engineering; Agricultural Economics and Rural Sociology and the Mushroom Test-Demonstration Facility although most staff members devote only a portion of their time to mushroom research.[31]

130. **What is the scientific name of mushroom study?** Mycology is a branch of botany dealing with fungi. Fungi are a group of saprophytic (live on dead matter) and parasitic (live on live matter) lower plants that lack chlorophyll and include molds, rusts, mildews, smut, mushrooms, and usually bacteria.

131. **How would I go about becoming a mycologist?** Mycologists major in agricultural or biological science with emphasis on microbiology, agricultural engineering and economics, and food science and technology. Contact Penn State University, University Park, Pa., 16802 for more detailed information.

Penn State University has a three-day Mushroom Industry Short Course in June of each year. It is open to anyone interested in mushrooms. Contact their Department of Botany for more information.

132. **Where can I obtain more technical information about commercial mushrooms?** A booklet entitled *Mushroom Growing and The Mushroom Industry,* 1977 revised edition—53 pages, is available for $2.50 from the American Mushroom Institute, Kennett Square, Pa., 19348. It includes a long list of books and college theses covering various mushroom subjects. It is written for people interested in learning how mushrooms are grown.

It tells technically about the commercial growing of spawn, making compost, pasteurization procedures, growing cycle, harvesting and marketing, diseases, pests, processing, costs, and recent economic developments and projections for the mushroom industry.

The *Fruit and Vegetable Facts and Pointers—Mushrooms,* June 1975, 22 pages, $1.80, published by United Fresh Fruit and Vegetable Assoc., 1019 19th St., N.W., Washington D.C., 20036. Much of what it contains is covered in this booklet you are reading. Its bibliography of 54 references might turn up an unknown source of information for you if you are making an in-depth mushroom study. It does not discuss the wild mushroom. (Incidentally, they have 77 other booklets on commodities from Anise to Watermelon. Price list and order form available upon request.)

Mushrooms and Penn State, Past, Present, Future—Robert Snetsinger, Bulletin 767, May 1970, 34 pages, History of growing mushrooms commercially, how it's done and the part Penn State has played in the mushroom field. This is a very interesting booklet, available at the office of county Agricultural and Home Economics Extension Offices in Pennsylvania or the Agricultural Mail Room, Agriculture Administration Building, University Park, Pa., 16802.

Manual of Mushroom Culture published and distributed by Mushroom Supply Co., Toughkenamon, Pa., 19374, over 225 pages and 150 illustrations, $6.00, by G. Raymond Rettew and Forrest G. Thompson, copyright 1948.

A Field Guide to Western Mushrooms, Alexander H. Smith, The University of Michigan Press, Ann Arbor, Michigan, 1975.

Non-Flowering Plants, Floyd S. Shuttleworth and Herbert S. Zim, Golden Press, New York, 1967 (paper and hard cover).

Mushrooms of North America, Osson K. Miller, Jr., E. P. Dutton, a Division of Sequoia-Elsevier Publishing Company, Inc., New York (soft and hard cover).

LOOSE ENDS

133.

Ants and termites were the first mushroom farmers.

A delicate mushroom is so powerful it can break cement sidewalks or asphalt streets or lift heavy rocks.

A mushroom eater is a Mycophagist.

Mushroom study provides a fascinating hobby as well as exercise.

Persistent winds stop the forming of wild mushrooms because they dry the ground.

Mushrooms, like monosodium glutamate, bring out the flavor of other things with which they are served.[29]

Of the 30,000 different world fungi, less than one percent are killers, which is a smaller proportion than among the flowering plants.[29]

It may take a hardwood stump 50 or 100 years to return to humus from the action of a succession of different species of mushrooms growing on it . . . some pine stumps may take several hundred years to decompose. They are not preferred hosts for fungi.[7]

More than 20 varieties of spawn are grown in France's cave farms.[11]

The Chester County Mushroom Laboratories, working with Wyeth, Inc., a pharmaceutical house, during the second world war, produced more penicillin in 1943, the first year of penicillin production, than any other laboratory in the world. Later other U. S. mushroom laboratories helped develop streptomycin.[25]

Modern mushroom culture produces more protein per unit area of land than any other form of agriculture.[14]

Mushroom soup has proven to be one of the best selling soups. The national advertising by soup companies has educated the people to enjoy the flavor and trust the quality of commercial mushrooms.[25]

U. S. commercial mushrooms are always picked before the veil breaks. In England, they prefer open mushrooms (broken veils.)[25]

U. S. commercial mushrooms' gill color goes from pink to dark brown, when the spores are released. The darkening color is caused by the development of the spores.[25]

No one can identify the different mushroom species by the spawn.[30]

Deadly poisonous and excellent edible species are the two extremes in mushrooms. Not many kinds are deadly and not many stand out as excellent edible species.[30]

Kennett Square, Pa. is known as the Mushroom Capital.

Edible mushroom species are known which can be cultivated at temperatures from 32° to 105° F.[14]

It is ironic that the United States has shipped large quantities of milk to developing nations to relieve protein deficiency, when those countries could have been taught to grow mushrooms and produce a continued supply of protein.[24]

According to James P. San Antonio, USDA Agricultural Research Service, it takes an approximate overall total of 5 to 8 tons (1,143 to 1,829 gallons) of water to grow one ton of mushrooms.

Mushroom growth and development depends more upon the soil temperature than that of the air. The darker, moist soil absorbs more heat than light dry soil.

Health food followers tell me that dandelion flowers, dredged in flour and then fried, taste like mushrooms.

RECIPES

134. What do I need to know about cooking mushrooms? The USDA recommends a serving size of 3 oz. of sliced, cooked mushrooms. Fresh mushrooms, cooked, yield 67% by weight after cooking. Three pounds contains approximately ten servings. 1 pound fresh buttons equals 4 cups sliced or 1⅓ cups sauted mushrooms.

Sauteed Mushrooms

Fry DRY mushrooms in a small amount of very hot fat in an open skillet. Do not pack them tightly together in the skillet or they will steam instead of fry. Never cover the pan and do not add extra fat. Shake the skillet occasionally to keep the best mushroom flavor, do not cook longer than 4 minutes.

Mushrooms in stews or casseroles should be added about 10 minutes before the finished cooking time or saute them separately and add to other ingredients just before serving.

Brown bag microwave lunch ideas

If your place of employment has an available microwave oven carry some raw sliced mushrooms with you to heat for lunch. For a sandwich slice an English muffin into two pieces, cover bottom half with butter, mushroom slices, paper thin onion slices, and cheese, cover with remaining muffin half. Do not overcook, the muffins will get tough.

Mushrooms in Sour Cream (from *Mushroom Cookery*)

An exotic vegetable to serve which couldn't be easier to make.

1 lb. mushrooms   salt and pepper
3 Tbsp. butter   fresh chopped parsley
        1 cup sour cream (½ pt.)

Use 1 pound of button mushrooms or halve large ones. Saute them in 3 Tbsp. of bubbly butter in a large skillet over moderately high heat for 3 minutes. Stir often.

Remove from heat and stir in 1 cup sour cream, which is at room temperature. Sprinkle with salt and pepper and serve garnished with freshly chopped parsley.

Stewed Mushrooms *(from Mushroom Cookery)*

1 lb. mushrooms   ½ tsp. salt
½ cup water   2 Tbsp. lemon juice

Bring ½ cup of water, ½ tsp. of salt, and 2 Tbsp. of lemon juice to a boil in a 2 or 3 quart saucepan. Add 1 pound of whole mushrooms and cover. Boil over moderate heat for 5 minutes, tossing them a few times. The lemon juice helps to keep them white.

The mushrooms should remain in their liquid until ready for use. If you wish to store, leave in liquid and place in a tightly covered container in the refrigerator (will keep for four days). Use their cooking liquid in a sauce, or reduce it by boiling and freeze the essence for later use.

Mushroom Chips (from *Mushroom Cookery*)

It is best to use large, firm mushrooms with closed caps for this dish. They make large slices. Even with the shrinkage that occurs, ½ pound of mushrooms yields enough chips to fill a quart bowl.

½ to 1 lb. mushrooms   1 cup oil   salt

Heat 1 cup of oil in a 1½ or 2 quart saucepan to 375°. Use a frying basket or perforated spoon for removing the chips from the oil.

Have the mushrooms at room temperature. Cold ones will cause the temperature of the fat to drop too quickly. Slice the mushrooms thin on the large blade of a vegetable grater.

To begin, drop some slices singly into the fat. They will start to brown and curl within 2 minutes. When browned, remove them to paper towels and sprinkle with salt. Drop a handful in next and stir with a fork to be sure they separate. When curled and browned remove to paper towels for draining. Salt them.

Continue frying a handful at a time. No more or they'll stick together. These are best served as soon as they're made, but they can be prepared in advance. Although they're good cold, they're crisper if heated on a cookie tin before serving.

Christmas Mushroom Salad (from *Mushroom Cookery*)
(good any time of year)

Combine Marinated Mushrooms, red cherry tomatoes, and fresh green broccoli buds in the marinade the mushrooms were cooked in. Not only is this a delicious and very pretty red-and-green salad, but it also has the advantage of gracefully maintaining its flavor and appearance even after sitting for many hours on an "open house" party table. It goes superbly with ham.

Broiled Mushroom Cheese Sandwiches

For each sandwich toast one side of bread (under broiler). Cover untoasted side with one slice of American cheese, paper thin onion slice and thinly sliced fresh mushrooms. Top generously with butter, broil 3 or 4 minutes or until mushrooms are hot and cheese bubbles.

Pickled Mushrooms

Bring Kraft Italian dressing to a boil in a saucepan, add cleaned mushrooms (small amount) and bring again to a full boil, boil 5 minutes. Drain mushrooms, return liquid to the saucepan. Repeat until all mushrooms are cooked. Combine mushrooms and liquid in a jar, cool, cover and store in refrigerator.

Mushroom Mayonnaise (from *Mushroom Cookery*)

This is an unusual mayonnaise. It can also be used as a dip. Because it is made in an electric blender, it doesn't take much time. As a dressing for a sliced fresh mushroom salad, it's perfect. Use it as you would any other mayonnaise.

¼ lb. mushrooms
2 eggs
1 tsp. salt
½ tsp. dry mustard
2 Tbsp. lemon juice
1½ cups oil

Break 2 whole eggs into an electric blender jar. Add 1 tsp of salt and ½ tsp. of mustard. Cover and blend for ½ minute at highest speed. (Use the highest speed throughout this recipe.) Add 2 Tbsp. of lemon juice and turn the blender on and off.

The oil should always be added in a thin slow stream, or in drops. Turn the blender on and begin adding the oil. After about ½ cup of oil has been added, the mayonnaise will begin to thicken and form a whirlpool in the center. Continue dripping the oil in and with the other hand drop a mushroom into the center of the whirlpool. If the mushrooms are large, cut them in half. Continue adding the oil slowly and continue adding the mushrooms, one at a time.

Do not add a mushroom until the last one has become incorporated into the mayonnaise. If the oil, or a mushroom, remains on top of the mayonnaise and the whirlpool has disappeared, replace the cover and turn the blender off. When you turn it on again, the whirlpool will again appear. Continue adding the oil and mushrooms until all are used. Refrigerate in a covered container and use cold. It will keep for almost a week. (Makes 3 cups.)

Boiled Mushrooms (from *Mushroom Cookery*)

Boiled caps are best for chilled stuffed mushrooms. They should be boiled in lemon water for 5 minutes and removed from the liquid immediately. Follow the directions for Stewed Mushrooms.

The advantage in using boiled mushrooms for stuffing is that they can be completely prepared in advance. They also lend themselves to elaborate garnishes, such as diamond-shaped truffles and petals cut from red pimento. Or they may be covered with aspic.

Cold stuffed mushrooms can be filled with cold salads, such as lobster, shrimp, crab meat, tuna, egg, ham, tongue, smoked oysters, etc. The stems should be boiled with the caps and chopped into the salads too. Serve clams or oysters in an uncommon way by placing them on boiled caps. Before adding the shellfish, place a spoon of cocktail sauce in the depression in the cap. Then garnish the top with a slice of lemon. An efficient and beautiful way to stuff cold mushroom caps is to force the filling through a pastry bag with a many-pointed tube.

Stuffed Mushrooms (from *Mushroom Cookery*)

Stuffed mushrooms can be used in a number of ways. The three best ways of preparing mushrooms to be stuffed: baking, boiling, broiling.

Stuffing must not be dry or it will fall apart, but it must not be soggy either. It must "handle well" as you place it into the cap.

Do not cut mushroom stems to remove them for stuffing, snap them to one side instead. This provides a depression in the center of the cap.

If possible, buy large mushrooms for stuffing. They may run from 12 to 20 to a pound. Very fresh, firm closed caps are heavier than open capped mushrooms with the gills showing. Open caps have lost moisture and are lighter in weight. They don't look quite as pretty, but they taste fine.

Baked Mushrooms (from *Mushroom Cookery*)

This is an easy method. Neither the caps nor the stems have to be cooked before baking. The mushrooms cook during the baking. Many cooks saute the stems first but this adds unnecessary fat to the stuffing. The moisture in the stems is released during the 15 minute baking period; this adds succulence. To reduce the raw taste of chopped onions, shallots, or scallions, some cooks like to saute them before they are added. However, if they are grated they automatically lose their raw taste during the baking time, and also add additional moisture, without extra fat. The concern with fat is to avoid a greasy taste, for it can overpower the delicacy of the mushroom, particularly when the mushrooms are no longer hot.

The following recipe for baked stuffed mushrooms is a good basic one. Use it as is or use it to elaborate on by adding ½ cup of cooked food, such as chopped shrimp or ham. No change is necessary, for the interior moisture is provided by the chopped stems and grated onion. The shredded cheese acts as a binder.

Baked stuffed mushrooms can be prepared in advance up to the point of baking. If they are stored in the refrigerator, they should be brought to room temperature before baking.

Basic Baked Stuffed Mushrooms (from *Mushroom Cookery*)

1 lb. large mushrooms
oil
½ cup fine bread crumbs
½ cup finely shredded Gruyère or Swiss cheese
4 Tbsp. grated onion and juice
½ tsp. chervil or tarragon
½ tsp. salt
pepper
2 Tbsp. (or more) milk, cream, or stock
bread crumbs
Parmesan or Romano cheese, grated
butter

Remove the stems from 1 pound of large mushrooms. Pour some oil into a bowl. With your fingers wipe some oil over the outside of each cap. Add a drop in the center of the inside, too, but don't add more oil once the first has become absorbed. Chop the stems fine, or use the easier technique of shredding them first and then chopping.

In a bowl combine the chopped mushrooms with ½ cup fine bread crumbs by tossing together with a fork. Add ½ cup finely shredded Gruyère or Swiss cheese and toss some more. Add 4 Tbsp. of grated onion and onion juice, ½ tsp. of chervil or tarragon, ½ tsp. of salt, and several turns of the pepper mill. Toss with fork again and add 2 Tbsp. of milk, cream, or stock. A little more may be needed to make the mixture moist enough so it holds together and doesn't crumble apart when it is handled.

Stuff the caps with the mixture. Round and smooth with your fingers. Sprinkle each cap with some bread crumbs and some grated Parmesan or Romano cheese, and dot each one with butter. Place the caps in a baking pan and bake in a preheated 375° oven for 15 minutes. If the caps are very large and heavy give them a couple of additional minutes baking time.

Baked mushrooms may be buttered instead of oiled. They may also be baked without being oiled or buttered if there is ½ inch of moisture in the baking pan. It can be milk, cream, stock, or sauce. The mushrooms must not be allowed to dry out.

Broiled Mushrooms (from *Mushroom Cookery*)

Remove the stems from the mushrooms. Pour some oil in a bowl and, using your fingers, oil the caps (or use softened butter if you prefer). Place the caps, round side up, under a preheated broiler, but not too close to the heat, about 3 or 4 inches away, and broil for 2 minutes. Turn the caps and broil the undersides for 2 minutes. Remove from heat and stuff them. Dot the tops with butter and broil again for about 4 minutes. They are ready when they begin to brown.

Remember, when broiling stuffed mushrooms, that the mixture doesn't cook very long. Therefore don't use ingredients which require more than 4 minutes broiling time.

Stuffed Mushrooms (Courtesy of Richard Deacon's Microwave Oven Cookbook, Thermador, 5119 District Blvd., Los Angeles, Ca.)

4 slices bacon, diced	1 (3 oz.) pkg. cream cheese
¼ cup minced onion	1 lb. fresh small mushrooms
2 Tbsp. minced green pepper	½ cup soft bread crumbs
½ tsp. salt	1 Tbsp. butter or margarine
½ tsp. Worcestershire sauce	

Combine bacon, onion, and green pepper in 4 cup measure. Cover with paper towel and cook by microwave for 4 minutes, stirring once.

Remove from microwave; pour off fat. Mix in salt, Worcestershire and cream cheese. Wash and dry mushrooms. Remove stems. Chop stems and add to bacon mixture. Fill mushrooms. In 2 cup measure, heat bread crumbs and butter in microwave for 1 minute; stir until well mixed. Press buttered crumbs on top of stuffed mushrooms. Place half the mushrooms in 6 x 10 inch baking dish, filling side up. Add ¼ cup hot water to baking dish and cook 2 minutes. Repeat with remaining mushrooms. Makes about 50.

WILD MUSHROOM RECIPES

Recipes with an asterisk(*) will also be good with commercial mushrooms.

Genera *Calbatia, Lycoperdon* (Puffballs)

Calvatia calbovista and *Lycoperdon*—Only young puffballs which have pure white meat should be used in cooking. Puffballs ripen rapidly so should be cooked soon after gathering. If they are even slightly yellow, they are no longer fit to eat. In cooking the *Calvatia* peel the skin if it appears tough. If small specimens are gathered, be sure to cut in half to make sure you do not have an *Amanita* button. The *Amanita* will show the outline of cap and stem, whereas the puffball will be solid white flesh. They are best preserved by freezing after sauteing, canning, and pickling (from *Wild Mushroom Recipes*).

Sauteed Puffballs (from *Wild Mushroom Recipes*)

Cut mushroom in ½ inch slices. Saute on medium heat in half olive oil and half butter. Turn slices. Cook about 5 minutes. Salt and pepper to taste.

French Fried Puffballs (from *Wild Mushroom Recipes*)

Cut mushrooms in ½ inch slices. Be sure they are dry. Fry in hot vegetable oil (375°). Cook 2-3 minutes. Drain on paper towels. Sprinkle with salt and pepper while still hot.

Genera *Helvella, Morchella, Verpa* (Sponge)

To clean morels and *Verpas,* cut off the bulbous end if it is especially dirty; quickly wash out the pockets, and dry. Care in picking eliminates lots of work here.

To clean *Helvellas,* it is best to trim as much of the dirt away as possible, then parboil and drain. Most of the dirt sinks to the bottom. What's left can be rinsed easily under running water. Dry thoroughly on paper towels.

Morels and *Helvellas* are best preserved by canning, sauteing before freezing, and drying (from *Wild Mushroom Recipes*).

Genus *Coprinus*

Coprinus—"Inky caps" mature and die in a day. It is best to refrigerate them immediately without washing, as washing hastens their deterioration. Even with refrigeration, they deteriorate hastily. They are best cooked by themselves. Discard the dark liquid given off from the mushrooms when cooking. A word of warning—alcoholic beverages should not be consumed while eating *Coprinus atramentarius* or soon after. Many people have suffered ill effects from this combination. To preserve, can only the very young buttom mushrooms in which the gills have not darkened (from *Wild Mushroom Recipes*).

Cream of Shaggy Mane Soup (from *Wild Mushroom Recipes*)

3 cups finely chopped Shaggy Manes
1 cup water
2 chicken bouillon cubes
1 inch cube of cheese (more if desired)
Dash of pepper
2 Tbsp. butter
1 Tbsp. flour
3 cups hot milk

In a 2 quart kettle, add mushrooms, water, bouillon cubes, cheese and pepper. Simmer together for about ½ hour.

Add butter blended with flour. Stir. Add milk. Bring to a boil for 1 minute to cook flour. Serve piping hot. 4-5 servings.

The above recipe, with more flour and less milk, makes a dandy creamed shaggy manes to serve over rice, noodles or biscuits (from *Wild Mushroom Recipes*).

Genus *Polyporus*

Polyporus sulphureus—In a young specimen, the flesh is soft and tender and the flavor mild. In an older specimen the meat becomes punky, tough and strong flavored. When preparing for the table, cut off 2 inches of the outer edge and use only this for cooking (from *Wild Mushroom Recipes*).

Stewed Sulphureus (from *Wild Mushroom Cookery*)

2 qts. mushrooms
1 cube butter
½ tsp. peppercorns
⅛ tsp. nutmeg
½ cup whipping cream
¼ cup flour
2 tsp. salt

Cook the mushrooms with the butter slowly in a double boiler 15 to 20 minutes AFTER they are heated through. To the juice of the mushrooms add the cream and thicken with the flour. Add spices and salt and heat till thickened and the seasoning has a chance to blend.

Fried Mushrooms *(Morels)***
(from *Amana® Radarange® Microwave Oven Cookbook*)

¼ lb. butter or margarine 12 large morel mushrooms
2 well-beaten eggs 1 cup cracker meal

Preheat 9½ inch Amana Browning Skillet 2½ minutes in Radarange Oven. Melt butter 1 minute. Dip mushrooms in eggs, and then cracker meal. Drain. Fry until golden brown in Radarange Oven 2 to 3 minutes. Turn halfway through cooking time. (Serves 4.)

MICRO-TIP: Fried mushrooms may be frozen, then reheated when needed on double thickness of paper towel.

FRENCH FRIED MUSHROOMS

Use closed mushrooms. The caps with exposed gills do not hold coating evenly. Mushroom coating can be either dry or a batter. For either heat oil to 375°. Cook only 5 or 6 mushrooms at a time, turning them once. When golden on both sides remove with a perforated spoon and drain on paper towels.

To dust, dampen mushrooms and shake them in a paper bag containing flour or a commercial dip mix. When dipping, shake excess batter from mushroom before dropping it into the oil.

To make batter use a commercial dip mix, for variety substituting beer for the liquid in their instructions. You can make your own batter, varying the seasonings to suit your taste, as follows:

BASIC BATTER

½ scant cup milk or beer
1 egg 1½ tsp baking powder
½ cup flour ¾ tsp salt

Mix all ingredients in a bowl and beat well. Use as is or add any of the following seasonings: pepper, onion powder, celery salt, hickory smoke salt, Parmesan cheese, ginger, nutmeg, paprika, rosemary, tarragon, oregano, marjoram, cayenne, Angostura bitters.

NOTE: Did you know that most restaurants serve frozen French fried mushrooms? This is why they taste different than ones you cook using fresh mushrooms.

Mushroom Fritters or Funnel Cakes*

To the basic French Fry batter add sauteed, finely chopped mushrooms. This is a good way to use stems. Use 1½ cups of chopped mushrooms fried in ½ Tbsp. of butter. Cool. Heat fat to 325°F. Combine mushrooms and batter. For fritters drop a tablespoon batter at a time into hot fat, for funnel cakes pour batter into a funnel or drizzle from bowl into the hot fat.

**Recipe courtesy Amana Refrigeration, Inc.

Onion Rings and Mushrooms (from *Wild Mushroom Cookery*)*

2 medium sized onions, peeled and
  sliced in ¼ inch slices
1 cup mushrooms   3 Tbsp. butter

Saute the onion rings in the butter until just softened. Add the mushrooms that have been cooked in a little water or in their own juice. Heat through and serve over slices of roast beef as a garnish.

Mushrooms and Macaroni (from *Wild Mushroom Cookery*)*

12 mushrooms   salt and pepper
2 Tbsp. butter   lemon juice
1¼ cups rich milk   dash of cayenne
  or white stock   ¼ cup grated cheese
2 Tbsp. flour   ¼ lb. cooked elbow macaroni

Saute mushrooms in the butter for about 6 minutes. Add the milk or stock and thicken with the flour. Cook the macaroni in salted water and drain. Combine with the mushrooms and milk or stock. Season with salt, pepper and lemon juice. When heated, stir in the grated cheese and cayenne.

Mushroom Chowder (from *Wild Mushroom Cookery*)*

6 slices of bacon,   1 cup water
  cut in small pieces   4 cups milk or light cream
1 small onion, chopped   salt and pepper to taste
1½ cups diced potatoes   chopped parsley for garnish
1½ cups mushrooms, chopped

Cook bacon and onion together very slowly until bacon is crisp and onions golden. Drain. Add the water, potatoes and mushrooms. Cook until the potatoes are tender. Add milk and salt and pepper. Heat to scalding. Do not boil.

Casserole of Rice and Mushrooms*
(from *Wild Mushroom Cookery*)

1 cup rice (uncooked)   ½ cup red wine
4 cups chopped mushrooms   2 tsp. salt
1 cup chopped onions   ⅛ tsp. pepper
½ cup butter   1 cup cooked green peas
3 cups chicken broth   ¼ cup grated Parmesan cheese

In a heavy skillet cook the rice, mushrooms and onions in the butter for 10 minutes. Pour into a heatproof casserole. Add wine, broth and seasonings, and mix carefully. Cover. Bake for 45 minutes to an hour until the rice is tender and all liquid is absorbed. Stir in the peas and sprinkle the cheese over the top. Put back in the oven uncovered until the peas are heated through and the cheese has browned.

MUSHROOM PANCAKE ROLL *(Wild Mushroom Cookery)* *

1 cup mushrooms, chopped
½ cup milk
2 Tbsp. butter
1 Tbsp. flour
½ tsp. salt

Saute the mushrooms in the butter for 5 minutes. Add the milk and salt. Thicken with the flour.

Make very thin pancakes and when they are done place a spoonful of the mushroom mixture on each one and roll up. Place side by side in a shallow heatproof baking dish. Sprinkle with Parmesan cheese and brown quickly.

MUSHROOM WINE SAUCE *(Wild Mushroom Cookery)* *

1 onion, finely chopped
1 cube of butter
1 lb. mushrooms, thinly sliced
1½ cups chicken consomme
1 cup dry white wine
1 Tbsp. flour

Saute the onion in the butter till wilted. Add the mushrooms and cook 5 minutes. Add the broth, wine, and the flour which has been stirred with a little of the broth until smooth.

Mushroom Catsup (like steak sauce)*
(from *Wild Mushroom Cookery*)

Use any mushroom of good flavor, being careful not to destroy the mushroom flavor with too much spice.

Layer sliced mushrooms in a crock with a sprinkle of salt between each layer. Next day crush the mushrooms with a wooden mallet. On the third day press through a colander lined with cheese cloth. Add to each quart of juice:

½ tsp. pepper   ⅛ tsp. nutmeg
¼ tsp. sweet marjoram   a dash of garlic salt (optional)

Boil for 15 minutes. strain through double cheese cloth. Boil again for 15 minutes on each of two following days. Bottle and seal in sterilized containers.

The American Mushroom Institute provides many small mushroom recipe booklets. A recent one entitled "Mushrooms go with Everything" included this unusual mushroom bread recipe which was baked in various sizes of mushroom shapes. They make unusual centerpieces which can be eaten. You might also want to varnish some for a permanent "bread art" centerpiece.

MUSHROOM BREAD

½ lb. fresh mushrooms or can (6 to 8 oz.) mushroom stems and pieces
5 Tbsp. butter or margarine, divided
1 cup finely chopped onion
2 Tbsp. brown sugar
1 Tbsp. unsulphured molasses
1 Tbsp. salt
¼ tsp ground black pepper
2 cups milk, scalded
1 egg
2 pkgs. active dry yeast
½ cup warm water
6 cups all-purpose flour, divided
2 cups toasted wheat germ
1 egg yolk
1 Tbsp. milk

Rinse, pat dry and finely chop fresh mushrooms or drain and chop canned mushrooms. In a large skillet melt 3 tablespoons of the butter. Add mushrooms and onions; saute 5 minutes; set aside. In a large mixing bowl combine remaining 2 tablespoons butter with sugar, molasses, salt and black pepper. Add milk. Stir until butter is melted; cool. Beat in egg. Dissolve yeast in water; stir into milk mixture. Add 3 cups of the flour and beat thoroughly. Add mushroom mixture, remaining 3 cups flour and wheat germ; blend. Turn out onto a generously floured board and knead until elastic, about 10 minutes, adding more flour if necessary. Place in a buttered bowl; cover and let rise in a warm place until doubled. Meanwhile, prepare pans for shaping mushroom bread. Use either three empty 1 pound coffee cans or two 1 pound 12 ounce cans from tomatoes or fruit or twelve 8 ounce tomato sauce cans. Cut out a circle from heavy cardboard 2 inches wider than the can opening. Trace size of can opening in center of cardboard circle; cut out and remove. Cover cardboard with aluminum foil. Place around open edge of can; grease can and foil. Punch down dough and fill cans about three-fourths full. In a warm place let rise until dough raises over top of can and begins to rest on cardboard lip forming the shape of a mushroom (smooth and shape dough with buttered fingers.) Mix egg yolk and milk. Brush over tops of breads. Bake in a preheated hot oven (400 F.) 35 to 40 minutes (25 to 30 minutes for small breads) or until browned and done. Remove from cans; cool. Bread may be shaped to fit into two 9 x 5 x 3-inch loaf pans and baked following preceding directions. Yield: about 4-3/4 pounds of shaped breads.

Mushroom Pie (from *Wild Mushroom Cookery*)*

2 cups cream
3 eggs well beaten
1 cup morels
4 slices bacon
1 cup Swiss cheese cubed

Heat the cream to scalding. Beat the eggs well and add to the cream. Saute the mushrooms in a little butter for 5 minutes. Fry out the fat of the bacon and crumble. Place the diced cheese, the bacon and mushrooms in an uncooked pie shell and carefully pour over them the egg and cream mixture. Bake in a moderate oven for 30 or 40 minutes. Cut in wedges to serve.

Mushrooms and Cream Cheese Sandwiches*
(from *Wild Mushroom Cookery*)

1 cup mushrooms after cooking
2 Tbsp. butter
1 Tbsp. water
1 (8 oz.) pkg. cream cheese
1 Tbsp. chopped chives
salt to taste

Cook the mushrooms in the water and butter. Add to the cheese with the chives and salt, and a little juice from the cooked mushrooms. Mix well and spread on toast or sandwich bread.

This can be thinned more and used as a dip with crackers or potato chips.

CRISP GOLDEN MUSHROOMS (American Mushroom Institute)

½ lb. small fresh mushrooms or 1 can (6 to 8 oz.) whole mushrooms
⅓ cup corn flake crumbs
½ tsp. Italian seasoning
¼ tsp. salt
Dash ground red pepper, if desired
¼ cup light cream or half and half

Rinse, pat dry and trim fresh mushrooms or drain canned mushrooms; set aside. In a small paper or plastic bag combine corn flake crumbs, Italian seasoning, salt and red pepper. Dip mushrooms into cream and then shake in bag with seasoned corn flake crumbs. Place on a cookie sheet. Bake in a preheated moderate oven (350 F.) 15 minutes. Serve as an hors d'oeuvre or main dish accompaniment.
YIELD: about 18 mushrooms.

Mushroom and Onion Shortcake (from *Wild Mushroom Cookery*)*

3 Tbsp. butter
1 thinly sliced onion
1¼ cup thinly
   sliced mushrooms
salt and pepper to taste
dash of paprika
dash of thyme
dash of powdered bay leaf
dash of mace
2 beaten eggs
¾ cup sour cream

Prepare recipe of baking powder biscuits or Bisquick. Roll out and press into a deep pie pan or shallow baking dish. Brush with melted butter.

Heat butter in fry pan, add onion and mushrooms. Cook over low heat, stirring constantly for 6 or 7 minutes. Season to taste with the spices. Spread evenly over the biscuit dough and pour over the eggs which have been blended with the sour cream. Bake at 350° for about 30 minutes, or until custard is firm on top. Serve hot.

Barbecued Mushroom Burgers**

(from *Amana® Radarange® Microwave Oven Cookbook*)

1 lb. ground beef
1 cup diced celery
1 chopped onion
2 (4 oz. each) cans sliced,
   drained mushrooms
2 tsp. chili powder
1 (10¾ oz.) can water
1 (10¾) oz. can condensed
   onion soup
½ cup catsup
3 Tbsp. quick-cooking tapioca

Combine beef, onion and celery in 1½ quart casserole. Cook in Radarange Oven 7 minutes. Stir halfway through cooking time. Add remaining ingredients. Stir well. Cook in Radarange Oven 8 minutes. Let stand, covered, 10 minutes before serving. (Serves 6-8.)
   MICRO-TIP: Serve on hamburger buns.

Mushroom Gravy (from *Wild Mushroom Recipes*)*

4 Tbsp. meat drippings
4 Tbsp. flour
2 cups water
2 chicken bouillon cubes
Small piece bay leaf
Soy sauce to color
Salt, pepper, Accent to taste
Sauteed mushrooms

On medium heat, add flour to meat drippings to make a roux. Add water, bouillon cubes and bring to a boil. Add bay leaf and soy sauce. Add salt, pepper, and Accent. Add sauted mushrooms.

Flavorful mushrooms to use in gravies are *Agaricus campestris, Armillaria ponderosa,* the Boletes, *Cantharellus cibarius* and *subalbidus, Marasmius oreades, Morchella esculenta, Sparassis radicata,* and *Clitocybe multiceps.*

**Recipe courtesy Amana Refrigeration, Inc.

Mushrooms Baked in Foil (from *American Mushroom Institute*)*

1 lb. fresh mushrooms or 2 cans (6 to 8 oz. each) whole mushrooms	2 Tbsp. minced onion 1 Tbsp. water or dry sherry 1 tsp. salt
¼ cup chopped parsley	⅛ tsp. ground white pepper

Rinse, pat dry and trim fresh mushrooms or drain canned mushrooms; place in center of a sheet of heavy duty aluminum foil. Sprinkle with remaining ingredients. Bring edges of foil up over mushroom mixture; crimp and seal. Place in a baking pan. Bake in a preheated moderate oven (350°F.) for 45 minutes or until mushrooms are cooked. YIELD: 6 portions.

Halibut Steaks with Mushroom Stuffing*
(from *American Mushroom Institute*)

¼ lb. fresh mushrooms or 1 can (3 to 4 oz.) mushroom stems and pieces	4 cup seasoned dry bread crumbs ¾ tsp. salt
6 Tbsp. butter or margarine, divided	2 Tbsp. lemon juice 1 egg, lightly beaten
¼ cup minced onion	2 (1¼ lb. each) halibut steaks

Rinse, pat dry and chop fresh mushrooms or drain canned mushrooms; set aside. In a medium saucepan melt 4 Tbsp. of the butter. Add onion; saute until transparent. Add mushrooms; saute 2 minutes. Remove from heat; stir in bread crumbs, salt, lemon juice and egg. Place one of the halibut steaks in a well-greased shallow baking dish. Spread stuffing over fish. Top with second steak. Dot with remaining 2 Tbsp. butter. Bake in a preheated hot oven (400°F.) 40 minutes or until fish flakes easily when tested with a fork. Garnish with sauteed sliced mushrooms and parsley, if desired. YIELD: 6 portions.

Skillet Mushroom Medley (from *American Mushroom Institute*)*

½ lb. fresh mushrooms or 1 can (6 to 8 oz.) sliced mushrooms	1 can (1 lb.) whole white onions, drained 1 green pepper, cut into strips
1 lb. sweet Italian sausage links	8 cherry tomatoes ½ tsp. salt
½ lb. frankfurters	¼ tsp. ground black pepper

Rinse, pat dry and slice fresh mushrooms or drain canned mushrooms; set aside. Cut sausage and frankfurters into 1 inch chunks. In a large skillet saute sausage until browned, about 10 minutes; add frankfurters and saute 5 minutes. Stir in reserved mushrooms along with remaining ingredients. Cook and stir for 8 minutes or until vegetables are hot. Serve from skillet, with toothpicks, as appetizers. YIELD: 8 to 10 appetizer portions.

BIBLIOGRAPHY

1. Albritton, Stanley, *Albritton's Standard Values in Nutrition and Metabolism. (Revised as Metabolism,* Philip L. Altman and Dorothy S. Dittmer, Federation of American Societies for Experimental Biology, 1968.)
2. Allegro, John M., *The Sacred Mushroom and The Cross,* Bantam Books, Hodder and Stroughton, Ltd., 1970.
3. ---, *Amana® Radarange® Microwave Cook Book, 1975,* Amana Refrigeration Inc.
4. Atkins, R., *Mushroom Growing To-Day,* Faber & Faber Ltd., 1961.
5. Bartelli, Ingrid, *Don't Pick Poison,* Cooperative Extension Service, Michigan State University, Extension Bulletin E-614.
6. Bartelli, Ingrid, *May is Morel Month in Michigan,* Cooperative Extension Service, Michigan State University, Extension Bulletin E-614.
7. Bartelli, Ingrid, *Mushrooms Grow on Stumps,* Cooperative Extension Service, Michigan State University, Extension Bulletin E-924.
8. Deacon, Richard, *Richard Deacon Microwave Cookbook,* Thermador/Waste King, 1974.
9. Esselen, Fitzpatrick, Brunnell, and Filios, *The Nutritive Value of Mushrooms,* University of Massachusetts, Massachusetts Agricultural Experiment Station, 1944.
10. Flanagan, G. Pat., *Beyond Pyramid Power,* DeVorss and Co., Santa Monica, California, 1975.
11. Kavaler, Lucy, *Mushrooms Moulds and Miracles,* George G. Harrap and Co., Ltd., 1967.
12. Kinrus, Aron, *Mushroom Growing and The Mushroom Industry,* American Mushroom Institute, August, 1977.
13. Kurtzman, Ralph H., USDA, Assorted Readings from *Proceedings of Seminar on Mushroom Research and Production,* Agricultural Research Council, Pakistan Press, Karachi, 1975.
14. Kurtzman, Ralph H., USDA, "Mushrooms as a Source of Food Protein" reprinted from: *Protein Nutritional Quality of Foods and Feeds,* Part 2., Marcel Dekker, Inc., New York, 1975.
15. Lapolla, Garibaldi, *The Mushroom Cook Book,* Funk & Wagnalls, 1967.
16. ---, *Mushroom Growing,* University of Wisconsin, Bulletin A 2670, February, 1976.
17. ---, "Mushroom Scientist Studies Mushrooms and Cholesterol," *Mushroom News,* July, 1975.

18. ---, *Mushrooms,* Crop Reporting Board, Statistical Reporting Service, USDA, Washington, D.C., August 1977.
19. ---, *Mushrooms,* U. S. International Trade Commission Publication 761, March 1976.
20. ---, *Mushrooms,* U. S. International Trade Commission Publication 798, January, 1977.
21. ---, "Unknown Frenchman Introduced Modern Cultivated Mushrooms," *The Packer,* Oct. 14, 1967.
22. Peppler, Henry J., editor, *Microbial Technology,* Universal Foods Corp., Milwaukee, Wisconsin, Reinhold Publishing Corp., New York.
23. Platt, Rutherford, *1001 Questions Answered About Trees,* Dodd, Mead and Co., 1959.
24. Reitz, Rosetta, *Mushroom Cookery,* Gramercy Publishing Co., Walker and Company, New York, 1945. (out of print)
25. Rettew, G. Raymond and Thompson, Forrest G., *Manual of Mushroom Culture, Mushroom Supply Co.,* Toughkenamon, Pa., fourth edition, 1948.
26. Rinaldi, Tyndalo, *The Complete Book of Mushrooms,* Crown, New York, 1972.
27. Sackett, Clarice, editor, *Fruit and Vegetables Facts and Pointers—Mushrooms,* United Fresh Fruit and Vegetable Association, June 1975.
28. San Antonio, James P., USDA, "Commercial & *Small Scale* Cultivation of the Mushroom *Agaricus bisporus* (Lange) Sing", reprinted from *Hortscience,* Vol. 10 (5), Oct. 1975.
29. Savondus, Moira, *All Color Book of Mushrooms and Fungi,* Crescent Books, Division of Crown Publishers, Inc., New York.
30. Smith, Alexander H., *The Mushroom Hunter's Field Guide,* The University of Michigan Press, Ann Arbor, Michigan, 1963.
31. Snetsinger, Robert, *Mushrooms and Penn State, Past, Present, Future,* The Penn State University, College of Agriculture, Agricultural Experiment Station, University Park, Pa., Bulletin 767, May 1970.
32. ---, *The Standard Cyclopedia of Horticulture,* Bailey, Macmillan Company, New York, 1963.
33. Watt and Merrill, "Composition of Foods", *Agricultural Handbook #8,* December, 1963.
34. ---, *Wild Mushroom Cookery,* The Oregon Mycological Society, Inc., 1973. (out of print)
35. ---, *Wild Mushroom Recipes,* Members of Puget Sound Mycological Society, Pacific Search, 1973.

INDEX
References are to question numbers

Agaricus bisporus, 15, 107
  average yield, 74
  classification, 10, 12
  colors, 19
  cultivated, 12, 21
  imports, 23, 83
  kits, 62
  white history, 19
Agaricus bitorquis, 16
Agaricus campestris, 12, 15, 107, 115, 117, 123
Amanita bisporigera, 123
Amanita muscaria, 122
  tree partner, 113
Amanita phalloides;
  Death cap, 15, 115, 117
  lethal dose, 123
Amanita verna, 123
Amanita virosa, 123
American Mushroom Institute, 61, 80, 84
Amino acids, 20
Armillaria mellea, Honey M.
  fox fire, 109
Artist's fungus, 127
Ascomycetes, 10
Auricularia auricula-judae, 16
Auricularia polytrical, 62

Basidiomycetes, 10
Beefsteak morel, 123
Bible, 126
Black coloration, 43
Botetus edulis, cepes, 21
  foreign translation, 24
  imported, 23
  tree partner, 113
Botulin, *Clostridium botulinum,* 81
Botulism, 80, 81
  food poisoning, 83
Bruising, 26, 29, 43
Buying motivation, 80

Calories, 38
Canada, 85
  U. S. Export data, 79
Canner-importers, 82
Canning, 47
Canning industry, 31, 52, 82, 84
  sales data, 79
Çap, pileus, 2
  cracks, 55
  identification, 89
  size, 28
Carpophore, 7
Casing, 63
Caves, 63
Cepes: see *Botetus edulis*
Chanterelle cibarius, 23, 121
  foreign translations, 25
Chester Country Mushroom Laboratories, 133
Chinese mushrooms, 58
Cleaning mushrooms, 32
Closed, mushrooms, 3, 39
Clostridium botulinum, 81
Collectors, 10, 39
Colors
  commercial species, 19
  wild identification, 89, 92
Compost
  cost, 70
  discarded, spent, 68, 69
  food value left, 71
  ingredients, 66
  ratio to mushrooms, 66
  recipe, 66
  reuse by mushroom farms, 68
  sunlight on, 55
Consumption, 48, 58, 79, 80
Conversion fresh-canned, 40
Cooking, 34
Coprinus comatus, shaggy mane, 93, 118
  alcohol reaction, 119

Cottage industry, 58
Culture; see mushroom
Cup, volva, 89, 123

Drying mushrooms, 49, 50, 51

Education,
    wild mushrooms, 86
Europe, 16
    mushrooms, 21
Exports, chart, 79
European, 21
    inspection, 105

Fairy Ring, 101
False morel, 123
Farm, mushroom
    history, 52
    locations, 56, 58
    number, 59
    tours, 76
    types, 63
First mushroom farmers, 133
Firsts, mushroom, 39
Flavor, wild, 53
Flush, 63
Fly Agaric,
    Amanita muscaria, 122
Flammulina velutipes,
    Enotake, 16
    kits, 62
Flats, 3, 39
Fox fire, *Armillaria mellea,*
    Honey mushrooms, 109
Freezing mushrooms, 46
Fruit; see mushroom
Flavor, 53
Flushes, 63
Fly amanita, 122
France, 23, 24, 25, 85
Function of mushrooms, 7
Future prospects, 58

Gills, lamelai, 2, 133
    identification, 89
Grade of mushrooms, 17

Growers, 84
Growing, wild
    locations, 14
    rate, 54
Growth rate, 54, 63
Gyromitra esculenta, false
    morel, beefsteak, 123
Gyromitra infula,
    false morel, 123

Health Inspectors,
    insecticides, 77
    raw food, 45
History of mushrooms, 52
Home grown mushrooms
    business, 61
    hobby, 62
Humidity, 26, 27
Hydroponics, 64

Identification, wild, 89
Imported mushrooms, 23
    canned, 85
    counter attack, 84
    effects on industry, 83
    powder, 50
    ratio of consumption, 79
Importers, 82
Insect
    eggs, 45, 49, 53
    evacuation, 97

Japan, 16, 21, 23, 85

Lactarius, 125
    tree partner, 113
Lamelai; see gills
Lentinus edodes; see Shiitake
Local species, 88
Light requirements, 55

Manure, 52, 66
Michigan State University
    bulletins, 88, 89
Microscope, 89, 126
Mines, 132
Miners' helmets, 75

Monomethylhydrazine, 123
Moon phases, 62
Morel, sponge, 15, 21, 93
  classification, 10
  false, 103
  grown commercially, 102
  true, 104
Mushrooms, commercial U. S. *(Agaricus bisporus)*
  beds, 55
  business organizations, 60
  Canners' Committee, 80
  capital city, 133
  classificaiton, 10, 12
  common names, 13
  confidence in, 133
  consumption, 48, 58, 79, 80
  cooking, 134
  cost, 31, 39
  culture, 6, 62
  demand, 52
  description, 1
  discoloration, 43
  industry, short course, 131
  kinds, 11
  kingdom, 12
  kits, 62
  literature, 132
  order, 12
  parts, 2
  plantings, 67, 74
  Processors' Assoc., 83
  Processors' Tariff Committee, 83
  purchase, 22
  purpose, 7
  spoilage, 26
  yield, 74
Mushrooms, other edible, 15, 16
Mushrooms, wild, 15
  cooking, 134
  home grown, 106
  keeping time, 96
  kits, 62

  picking, 95
  protecting yourself, 94
  for beginners, 93
  sale laws, 105
Mutsutake, 21
Mycelium, spawn, roots,
  threads, 4, 6, 7, 52, 57, 58, 63, 110, 111
  fairy ring, 101, 102
Mycologia, 87
Mycological collections
  labeling, 91
Mycological Society, 87
Mycological Society of America, 87
Mycologist, 131
Mycology, 130
Mycophagist, 133
Mycorrihiza, 1, 110, 111, 112, 113
Mystery cult, 126

McIlvanea, 87

Nameko, 16
Near East mythology, 126
Nitrogen,
  liquid, 46
  used compost, 71
  protein, 20
North American Mycological Association, 87, 89
Nycophile, 87
Nutrition, breakdown, 20

Omphalotus illudens, 109
Opens, 3, 39
Organically grown, 77
Oriental, 16, 21
  production, 58
Oxydizing enzyme, 43
Oyster mushroom, 16, 58, 62

Packaging, 29
Pan, cooking use, 36
Padi straw mushrooms, 16

Panaeolus subbalteatus, 122
Parasitic, 1, 111
Pasteur Institute, 123
Peeling mushrooms, 32
Penicillin, 133
Pennsylvania, 56, 65, 66, 82
Pennsylvania State University
    Horticulture Dept., 84
    Research 52, 84, 129, 131
Pesticides, 77
Pholiota nameko, Nameko, 16
Picking mushrooms, 63, 72
Pileus; see cap
Pinhead, 3, 54
Poison Fungi Center, 120
Poisoning, 118
    after symptoms, 120
    eating, 114
    inhaling, 114
    symptoms, 118, 119
    ways, 118
Poisonous
    information, 121
    killers %, 133
    lethal dose, 123
    mind-altering drugs, 122
    mistakes, 117
    most deadly, 123
    reputation, 126
    serum, 123
    tests, 116
    touching, 114
    your only protection, 115
Powder, 50, 51
Preserving, 39, 46 47, 48, 49,
    50, 51
Primitive tribes, 125
Propagation, 57
Protein, 133, 20
Psalliota avbensis, 12
Psilocybe family, 122
Ptomaine poisoning, 118
Puffballs, 15, 93
    tree partner, 113

Rat study, 20
Raw mushrooms
    commercial, 34
    raw, 45
Recipes, 134
Religious superstitions, 126
Reproduction, 6, 62
Research Laboratories, 128
Research results, 20, 129
Roots; see mycelium

Sales chart, 79
Sales cooperative, 60
Saprophytic, 1
Season, mushroom, 18
Seasonings, 37
Seconds, 39
Seeds; see spores
Shaggy mane, 15, 93, 118, 119
Shape varieties, 92
Shiitake, 16, 21, 23
    kit, 62
Shrinkage, 41
Size, best, 28
Slicing, 33
Soaking, 32, 35
Soup, history, 133
Spawn; see mycelium
Species epithel, 10
Spoiled, 44
Spore, 4, 6
Spore print, 6
    how to make, 90
Sporophore, 7
Stages, 4
    fruit, 4, 7
    growth, 3
    mycelium, 4, 6, 7
    spores, seeds, 4
Stalk, 2
Stem, 2
    Amanita, 123
    discarding, 42
    identification, 89

Stipe, 2
Store packaging, 29
Storing, 27
Strains, 78
Stripping a wild area, 100
Stumps, 133
Subdivision, fungi, 12
Sulphur polypore, 93
Symbiotic, 1

Taiwan, Republic of China, 16, 23, 85
Temperature, 6, 18, 26, 30, 31, 39, 43, 48, 49, 133
   discoloration cause, 54, 63
Texture, 1, 9, 16, 28, 46
Threads; see mycelium
Trays, 55
Toadstools, 8

U. S. Dept. of Agriculture
   chart, sales, 79
   Crop Reporting Board, 65
   mushroom grades, 17
   Western Reg. Research, 107, 128
   Northeastern Reg. Research, 54, 66, 67, 68, 69, 71, 73, 74
   Poison Fungi Center, 120

U. S. Dept. of Commerce, 85
U. S. Food & Drug Adm.
   investigation, 81
   recall, 83
U. S. International Trade Comm., 83
University of Massachusetts, 20
University of Michigan, 94
University of Minnesota, 93

Vacuum cooling, 30
Vegetable, 5
Veil, allulus, 2, 133
Volva, 2

Water,
   canning, 48
   content of mushroom, 31, 41
   growth requirements, 6, 18, 54, 133

You may order additional
ANSWERS TO YOUR MUSHROOM QUESTIONS PLUS RECIPES
by mailing $3.95 plus 75c each for handling and postage. Michigan residents please add 4% sales tax. All Canadian orders please use a U.S. Funds money order for $3.95 plus $1.05 handling and postage.

The Mushroom Cave, Inc.
Post Office Box 894
Battle Creek, Michigan 49016
Telephone 616-962-3497